THE PROPHETIC

DESTINY OF ISRAEL

&

THE ISLAMIC NATIONS

DR. BILL SHADE

The Prophetic Destiny of Israel & the Islamic Nations

By Dr. Bill Shade

Printed in the United States of America

Copyright © 2014 by Dr. Bill Shade

Unless otherwise indicated, Bible quotations are taken from the King James Version of the Bible

ISBN-13: 9781499712193
ISBN-10: 1499712197

GLOBE

PUBLISHERS

Dedicated to all those
Whose hearts burn within them
To know the wonders
Of The Book

CONTENTS

FOREWORD:

Backgrounds: Why I Wrote This Book

I was in Europe shortly after the iron curtain came down and the Berlin wall fell and I was asked, "How will the events of these last few months change your understanding of prophecy, especially concerning Russia and the Middle East?" I answered that it would make no change at all. While it is legitimate to view current events through the lens of the prophetic Scriptures, it is like looking through the wrong end of a telescope to interpret prophecy by looking at current events. The prophetic Scriptures do not change with the shifting sands of political movements.

I fear, however, that some of us may have forgotten that principle. Suddenly, with fast-paced changes in the world's political landscape, and especially with the resurgence of militant Islam, prophetic students have begun to change long held and carefully crafted prophetic interpretations to bring them more in line with what is perceived to be current realities. "Mystery Babylon" now becomes to many literal Babylon, Mohammed becomes the Anti-Christ and Islam becomes the great whore of the Revelation.

While we must always remain willing to reverse formerly held positions when compelled by further study of the Scripture to do so, we must also guard against the temptation to be *soon shaken in mind, or be troubled, by spirit, or by word, or by letter* as Paul clearly warned the Thessalonian believers.

It is my conviction that the prophetic voice of the Scriptures is clear and that they speak to both the future of the nation Israel and to that of the Islamic nations as well. Yes, Israel has a future, and so do those nations that vehemently oppose her.

Opposition to Modern Israel
As I did research for this book, I was shocked by the number of opposing voices that are currently being raised against Israel and against her restoration as a nation. There is a growing chorus of church leaders who claim the label "Evangelical", that are

decidedly opposed to the views expressed in this book. As I searched the web for related information, I encountered page after page of angry diatribes against Israel and against those who support her. Perhaps that reaction should not be unexpected, since we in the evangelical camp seem to be muddling through a major shift in both philosophy and theology.

Post Modernists question the very existence of a metanarrative in History. Emergent leaders speak of the Rapture as "Pop evangelical theology." A new generation of Reformed teachers are returning to a non-descript Amillennialism accompanied by a rejection of modern day Israel. The Rapture of the Church, the future of Israel and the Millennial Reign of Christ are all strongly under attack at the very time when all the pieces of that prophetic puzzle are coming together as never before.

Just recently a branch of the Presbyterian Church in the USA published a study guide entitled *Zionism Unsettled*. It is probably the most frontal and direct attack on the restoration of Israel that has been published by a denominational group.

***Susan Michael is US Director for International Christian Embassy Jerusalem** and creator of **www.IsraelAnswers.com**.* She wrote a response to the study guide in an article posted February 19, 2014 by **Jerusalem Connection**. Because of the nature of this current debate, I am reproducing a portion of it here:

> "A disturbing study guide entitled "Zionism Unsettled" has been published by an arm of the Presbyterian Church (U.S.A.) The publication is filled with distorted facts and a historical narrative so extreme that some Jewish groups are calling it "hate speech." . . . The study guide proves that the PCUSA has aligned itself with the most radical of positions. . .
>
> The Chapter on "Evangelicals and Christian Zionism" skews the facts to portray Christians who support Israel as dangerous and a threat to Middle-

East peace. The chapter is taken largely from the writings of Dr. Gary Burge, an evangelical Presbyterian and Professor of New Testament at Wheaton College, who admits to holding a form of Replacement Theology.

The PCUSA has also aligned itself with extreme and radical groups such as *Sabeel* (an organization founded by Naim Ateek). Sabeel propagates Palestinian Liberation Theology that disregards any portion of scripture that disagrees with Ateek's anti-Semitic views. Hence, right out of the Sabeel playbook, <u>this study guide calls for churches to stop using hymns and liturgy that use the biblical terms: exodus, covenant, return, blossoming of the desert, Zion and Israel</u>.

It is time that the PCUSA wakes up and realizes that holding radical and anti-Semitic positions, such as reflected in this study guide, will only guarantee their continued membership decline, because most Americans not only shun hate speech, but admire and stand with the people of Israel. 1

In her article Susan mentions Naim Ateek.   The Rev. Dr. Naim Stifan Ateek is a Palestinian priest in the Anglican Church, a former Canon of St. George's Cathedral, Jerusalem, who lectures widely both at home and abroad.   He is founder of the *Sabeel Ecumenical Liberation Theology Center* in Jerusalem.   In December 2009, Sabeel endorsed the *Kairos Palestine Document* (KPD), which calls on Christians throughout the world to join the 2005 call of Palestinians to utilize boycotts, divestment, and sanctions to pressure Israel's government to end "occupation", "human rights violations", and "illegal settlement of Palestinian land". Dr. Ateek has been an active leader in the shaping of the Palestinian liberation theology.

Sabeel assumes the position that the Land Israel now occupies does not belong to her and therefore calls on the world to punish Israel for occupying it. Terms such as, "the occupation," or "the west bank", are only valid if you believe the Land belongs to someone beside Israel.

It is all the more tragic in my view, that the theological formulatiion for this comes from the Professor of New Testament at Wheaton College, Dr. Gary Burge. Dr. Burge is a Presbyterian who ascribes to a form of Replacement Theology which teaches that God has abandoned the Jewish people, and will fulfill His promises to them with the new "Spiritual Israel" the Church. It is this very doctrine that was the rational for centuries of Christian anti-Semitism and persecution of the Jewish people. This doctrine was concocted by Rome in the days of Augustine and has tragically resurfaced in much of the new Reformed Theology of our day.

In a similar vein there is the voice of Dr. Stephen Sizer who is the Vicar of Christ Church in Virginia Water, Surrey, England, and the author of *Christian Zionism: Road-map to Armageddon?* (InterVarsity Press, 2004) In Dr. Sizer view, "Christian Zionism (i.e., those Christians who are favorable toward Israel and believe in her national destiny), is the largest, most controversial and most destructive lobby within Christianity. It bears primary responsibility for perpetuating tensions in the Middle East, justifying Israel's apartheid colonialist agenda and for undermining the peace process between Israel and the Palestinians."2 Not surprisingly Dr. Sizer is the featured speaker at a *"24 Hour Middle East Leadership Briefing"* to be held at Wheaton College and – hosted by Dr. Gary Burge.

Another popular promoter of Anti-Israel Theology is Charles (Chuck) Carlson (not to be confused with Chuck Colson). Charles Carlson is Chief Executive Officer of Horizon Publishing, an investment newsletter publisher. Carlson, who was once aligned with an independent dispensational church, writes in web page http://charlesecarlson.com/ about his, "openly and publicly challenging many dispensational, "Christian Zionist churches". . . to their prevalent blindness to the plight of the Palestinians." Carlson's means of "challenging" them is by organizing noisy and confrontational marches and boycotts outside any church that sponsors a meeting on behalf of Israel. Carlson defines Christian Zionism as, "the contrived (sic) belief that, the modern political state of Israel is the fulfillment of Biblical Prophesy." 3

In a slide show advertised on his website, Carlson blames C. I. Scofield and the Scofield Reference Bible for the beginnings of Zionism. It is obvious Carlson is a little short on the facts of history as I will seek to show later in this Foreword. Carlson argues that supporting Israel means supporting killing of Palestinians. It is not too surprising then, that Carlson is often cited favorably on Al-Jazeerah, CCUN, the Arab News channel.

The Dual Covenant Proponents

At the other extreme of this debate there is a growing number of evangelical groups that are committed to supporting national Israel, but who actually cross the line of Biblical truth and teach that Jews do not have to come to Christ in order to be saved – they believe the Judaic covenants are sufficient for them. The position is called *Dual Covenant Theology.*

According to the on line dictionary Wikipedia, "Dual-covenant theology is a Christian view of the Old Covenant which holds that Jews may simply keep the "Law of Moses", because of the "everlasting covenant" (Genesis 17:13) between Abraham and God, whereas Gentiles must convert to Christianity to be assured of a place in the World to Come." Unfortunately there is evidence that this has become the position of some particularly within the Charismatic Movement.

Dr. John Hagee, whom we applaud for supporting Israel, nevertheless steps over this line in a recent U-tube advertisement for his new book, *In Defense of Israel*. Dr. Hagee said:

> "This book will expose the sins of the fathers and the vicious abuse of the Jewish people. 'In Defense of Israel' will shake Christian theology. It scripturally proves that the Jewish people as a whole did not reject Jesus as Messiah. It will also

prove that Jesus did not come to earth to be the Messiah. It will prove that there was a 'Calvary conspiracy' between Rome, the high priest, and Herod to execute Jesus as an insurrectionist too dangerous to live. Since Jesus refused by word and deed to claim to be the Messiah, how can the Jews be blamed for rejecting what was never offered?" 4

Thus is one paragraph Dr. Hagee denies that Jesus ever made a valid offer of the Kingdom to Israel (a fact that the Gospel of Matthew was written to establish), or that Jesus claimed to be the promised Messiah (something his miracles and resurrection prove and which he himself affirmed in John 4:25, 26), or that Israel rejected Jesus Christ and called for His crucifixion (which all the Gospels clearly record) – quite a list of denials of basic Christian teaching in one paragraph. Dr. Hagee does not "shake Christian theology", he abandons it.

As a result of this aberrant theology, Hagee has been cited as believing the Jews do not have to accept Jesus Christ in order to be saved – they are saved by the Abrahamic Covenant. Charisma Magazine took issue with him (without naming him) in an article entitled, *The Dangers of Dual Covenant Theology.* Author Jonathan Bernis wrote,

> "I recently heard one prominent leader (who I otherwise greatly respect) say, 'Jews do not come to Christ through proclamation, but through revelation.' Apparently, this leader feels it is God's job to reveal Himself to Jewish people despite Christ's command to make disciples of all men. Although his point of view is not exactly dual covenant theology, the result is the same-there is no need to share our faith with Jewish people." 5

So here we have the other extreme side of this debate. One denying that ethnic Israel has any prophetic future at all, and the other declaring that Israel does not need spiritual conversion – she is already right with God. The concerted voice of the Old Testament prophets as well as the New Testament Epistles would most certainly challenge that. Between these two false extremes, I believe there is a middle ground of truth that not only has Biblical support, but a whole company of historic champions who have laid hold on the hope set before Israel.

A Historic Position

Dr. David Larsen, who earned his B.A. from Stanford University, his M.Div from Fuller Theological Seminary; and his D.D. from Trinity College, and continues to hold the chair of Professor Emeritus of Preaching at Trinity Evangelical Divinity School, has written a book entitled **Company of Hope**. In it, he traces the history of the premillennial position from the first Century to the present.

Beginning with the teaching of the O.T. Prophets, our Lord Himself and the Apostles, Dr. Larsen moves through the first several centuries with names like Hippolytus, Clement of Rome, Ignatius of Antioch, Justin Martyr, Irenaeus and Tertullian.

Dr. Larsen is not the last to recognize the vast company of those who have held to a millennial expectation. From the website, **Israel Answers,** comes a similar record under the heading, **Christian Zionists Hall of Fame**. Because of the length of the list, I have placed a portion of it in the Appendix (see Appendix II).

While Premillennial Dispensationalists may not be a majority voice, they have had and continue to have a very important voice in framing the Church's understanding of the future and especially God's program for the nation Israel. If the dissenters wish to distain us, let them do so, but we are not ashamed of either our total abandoned loyalty to the Scriptures, our careful exegesis of its inspired words, or the companies of those who have lead us to the truth we presently embrace.

It is that truth I want to expand upon as we examine that most crucial subject of Israel's future destiny, particularly her restoration and conversion and subsequently, the destiny of those

Islamic Nations who have made themselves her enemies. In doing so let me make several disclaimers. First, I am not blind to the faults of National Israel and am under no illusion that there are and have been wrongs committed by both Israel and their Arab neighbors. I am certainly not ready to defend every action Israel takes.

However, critics need to remember that when the Balfour Declaration was first drawn and accepted by the then League of Nations, all of what is today the country of Jordan and all of what lies west of the Jordan river was proposed as a country to be given for Jewish habitation. All of that territory was, at that time, without national boundaries and had been for centuries merely existing as a part of the vast Ottoman Empire. But before the Jews were given permission to own this vast "land without a people" the League of Nations took away the 38,000 square miles of territory lying east of the Jordan River and created the modern state of Jordan as a gesture of good will to the Arabs. The remaining approximately 8,000 square miles west of the Jordan was committed to the Jews.

However, just before Israel attained statehood, the remaining land was divided (once again to appease the Arabs), along lines that were disconnected and completely indefensible. In spite of this blatant betrayal and reversal of all that the original planners had promised and envisioned, Israel accepted the terms, but the Arab countries immediately attempted to eliminate Jewish Israel altogether.

I have carefully followed the wars and movements that have followed and find myself giving ascent to Golda Mier's words, "If the Arabs would lay down their arms there would be no more war. If Israel would lay down her arms, there would be no more Israel." To speak of Israel as the aggressor is strangely inconsistent, when all that she is trying to do is to occupy what Abba Eban, their former Foreign minister once called, "The narrowest territory in which Israel's national purposes can ever be fulfilled?" (See full statement in the Appendix I)

In addition, I have no illusions about Israel's present spiritual state. I believe God is at work in Israel and that she is being prepared for a time when she will meet her long rejected Messiah, Jesus Christ and receive Him as her own. That meeting has yet to come for most of the nation remains in stubborn unbelief toward the claims of Jesus Christ. But meet Him she must, for there is no salvation apart from Him. The Bible's message is: *Testifying both to the Jews and also to the Greeks, repentance toward God and faith toward our Lord Jesus Christ* (Acts 20:21).

Of course there is also the Islamic Nations that surround Israel on every side. What of them? What is their future destiny? Well, Islam has an eschatology, but it conclusions are completely different from those of the Scripture.

So in this crucial time, when some deny any prophetic validity to national Israel, and others deny the need for her to come to a faith relationship with Jesus Christ, and many more question what the outcome of Islamic militancy will be, I have come to the conclusion that there has never been a more important time to address each of those issues in a way that will look at the promised national restoration of Israel and her spiritual conversion and the fate of that system and those nations which oppose her. The following pages seek to achieve that goal.

INTRODUCTION:

It was a beautiful sunny Sunday morning and the refreshing breeze was blowing briskly up the hill from the Sea of Galilee (also known as Kinneret, Lake of Gennesaret, or Lake of Tiberias), to the Kibbutz where my tour group were staying. After breakfast we would journey the short distance down to the town of Tiberius and then board our tour ship for a trip across the approximate eight miles of lake that lay between us and the base of the Golan Heights.

As we departed from Tiberius seated on the open deck of our small ship we held a brief service of song and worship and I began to bring a message from Ezekiel about the future conversion of Israel to Yeshua Hamashia and the events which would trigger it. I turned in the Scripture to Ezekiel's description of the northern invasion, it seemed at times we could almost see the combined armies the prophet names in his vision as they ravished over the verdant hills surrounding the lake. I explained how Israel would at last realize their helpless plight before the aggressors and be driven to cry out in repentance to God for His intervention and mercy.

I spoke of how, in the hour Israel cries out to the One they had rejected and pierced, the Holy Spirit would open long blinded eyes to the One and only Redeemer. Israel's "heart transformation" is promised by God in chapter thirty six of Ezekiel and visualized in chapter thirty seven. Chapters thirty eight and thirty nine reveal the conditions and events that will bring it to pass.

My message that morning was necessarily long and I only finished as we approached our landing dock on the eastern shore of the lake. As we disembarked, the crew of our tour ship approached me, led by their Captain. As they neared me I realized that the captain, a refugee from Germany and a survivor of Hitler's holocaust, was weeping. Without hesitation the old man threw his arms around my neck and whispered, "Oh, I hope dat all you said is true." After repeating it several times I reminded him that I had taken it directly from his own Scriptures, but he could only repeat again those same words, "Oh, I hope dat all you said is true."

It is because it is true that I have taken up my pen to examine it here. God never says Whoops! He did not create the earth and decree that man should have dominion over it, only to be frustrated by man's abrogation of his sovereignty to Satan. He did not create man to have fellowship with Himself and then never realize the goal because of man's sinful fall and subsequent alienation. He did not choose Abraham and his seed and establish great unconditional covenants with him, only to have to leave Israel on the ash heap of history because of human failure. God is greater than that – He is wiser than that – and He never says Whoops!

The study we are about to undertake will show that God intends to fulfill every promise, realize every goal, bring to fruition every decree, and glorify Himself, His wisdom, His justice and His grace through it all. With all our knowledge of prophetic events, the one thing that seems to elude most writers is not the fact of Israel's conversion - God has guaranteed that in the New Covenant - but the timing and the event that will set it in motion. When will it happen and what events will transpire that will bring it to pass and what will be the fate of those who oppose her? That is the subject of this book.

SECTION ONE:

THE

CERTAINTY OF

ISRAEL'S

FUTURE CONVERSION

Chapter One - Establishing a Rational

When we talk about the Conversion of Israel, we actually mean that time when Israel, as a nation (or in large number), will repent and turn in faith to their Messiah and Savior, Yeshua (Jesus). Perhaps the idea may seem a bit strange to any who are familiar with the present attitude of much of that nation toward Jesus Christ. Are we who talk of spiritual conversion for Israel trapped in wishful thinking? Are we simply illusionary?

The essence of Faith is taking God at His word, especially when all of the external evidence seems to the contrary – *"Hope that is seen is not hope, for what a man seeth, why doeth he yet hope for? But if we hope for that we see not, then do we with patience wait for it"* (Romans 8:24, 25).

It was that faith that drove the words of C. H. Spurgeon, when discoursing on the meaning of Ezekiel's vision of the Valley of Dry Bones, Spurgeon said;

> The meaning of our text, as opened up by the context, is most evidently, if words mean anything, first, that there shall be a political restoration of the Jews to their own land and to their own nationality; and then, secondly, there is in the text, and in the context, a most plain declaration, that there shall be a spiritual restoration, a conversion in fact, of the tribes of Israel. 6

Although there is a growing body of evidence that suggests that God is at work in Israel today, it is not the external evidence that drives us to the conclusion that Israel's future is bright and that her conversion is certain. Rather it is our absolute confidence in the veracity and immutability of God and His covenant promises. That is the line of evidence I want to begin with and examine – the covenant promises of God to Israel.

The Unconditional Covenants

God made four great unconditional covenants with the nation of Israel that are recorded in the Scripture. These are, the Abrahamic Covenant (Genesis 12:1 – 3), the Palestinian Covenant (or Land Covenant – Genesis13; 15; 17; 22; 26; 28), the Davidic Covenant (or Seed Covenant – 2 Samuel 7), and the New Covenant (or Blessing Covenant – anticipated in Deuteronomy 30:6; fully revealed in Jeremiah 31:31 – 37). Please note that these are not assumed or contrived "theological covenants," the kind that so many seemed to be enamored with just now, but these are stated, Biblical covenants, clearly revealed and initiated by God.

As you will observe by closer examination, the original Covenant with Abraham has three distinct promises. God promised Abraham the Land (Genesis 13:14 – 18), a Seed (Genesis 15:1 – 6), and a Blessing (Genesis 22:15 – 18). The three additional covenants, are specific expansions upon each of those three aspects of the original Covenant with Abraham.

The Abrahamic Covenant

Before examining any of the provisions of the covenants, I want to examine the reason we refer to all of them as unconditional covenants. Consider carefully the wording in each of the following passages all of which will refer to the foundational Covenant with Abraham:

> *Now the LORD had said unto Abram, Get thee out of thy country, and from thy kindred, and from thy father's house, unto a land that I will shew thee: And I will make of thee a great nation, and I will bless thee, and make thy name great; and thou*

shalt be a blessing: And I will bless them that
bless thee, and curse him that curseth thee: and in
thee shall all families of the earth be blessed
(Genesis 12:1 – 3).

It must be at once obvious that this entire covenant rests solely upon the Sovereign *I Will* of God.   Upon Abraham's departure from his own country God instituted with Him this covenant in which He specifically promises three things; a land to live in, a seed (*make of thee a great nation*), and a universal blessing that would come upon Abraham and through Abraham and his seed to all the earth.

In the very next chapter of Genesis (Chapter 13), Abraham separated from Lot. In a gracious gesture entirely unique to an eastern culture – Abraham (the elder), deferred to Lot (the younger). Such a thing is unheard of even today in eastern culture – Abraham giving Lot the honor of the choice of the land.

As we examine the life and legacy of Abraham we will discover that this is not an isolated action on Abraham's part. It is, rather, a pattern that is traceable throughout his life, and in each instance where Abraham sacrifices what is naturally his, and yields his rights to another, at that very point God meets him and pours on him an ever expanded blessing. I think it would be helpful to trace that pattern.

In Chapter twelve Abraham left his security and his people in Ur to follow God, and God gave the promises of the Covenant to him (Genesis 12:1 – 3). In his conflict with Lot, he yielded the best of the land and God promised him all of it (Genesis 13:8, 9).   In chapter fifteen he gives back all that he has taken in battle and God becomes both his protection and his treasure, *I am thy shield and thy exceeding great reward* (Genesis 15:1). In chapter twenty two Abraham reaches the pinnacle of surrender in giving his very own son to God and God promises to extend blessing through Abraham to *all the nations of the earth* (Genesis 22:18).

What a lesson for us all. No one can out-give God. The more we give up, the more God blesses. At every point of surrender God will meet us with *more than we could ask or think* – and that is not some kind of prosperity gospel – that is the well established experience of God's people through the ages.

I have taken the liberty of putting these Scripture passages here in print because they are essential to our discussion. I could have simply given a reference for them, but experience tells me that the reader will not often bother to look up those references and hence the force of the Scripture itself is lost to the discussion and in this discussion, it is too important to loose.

While there is no doubt merit in referencing what others have said, and I have read much that has been written, my appeal will be primarily to the Scriptures themselves – hence the number and length of the references.

> *And the LORD said unto Abram, after that Lot was separated from him, Lift up now thine eyes, and look from the place where thou art northward, and southward, and eastward, and westward: For all the land which thou seest, <u>to thee will I give it, and to thy seed **for ever**</u>. And I will make thy seed as the dust of the earth: so that if a man can number the dust of the earth, then shall thy seed also be numbered. Arise, <u>walk through the land in the length of it and in the breadth of it; for I will give it unto thee.</u>* (Genesis 13:14 – 17)

Thus God blesses Abraham as he separates from Lot. Notice the underscored words: *I will give it forever . . . I will give it unto thee.* The Land was God's gracious gift to Abraham and to his seed in perpetuity.

As noted above, the next instance of God expanding His promise to Abraham follows his renunciation of the spoils of war and the giving of his tithe to the *Priest of the Most High God* — Melchizedek.   In the midst of a strange country, bereft of the protection he might have gained by keeping his captives, or the wealth he might have had by keeping the spoil, Abraham gives up both and abandons himself to God. However, it is that very act of faith that allows him to challenge God about the promises of both a seed and the Land.

> After these things the word of the LORD came unto Abram in a vision, saying, Fear not, Abram: <u>I am thy shield, and thy exceeding great reward.</u> And Abram said, Lord GOD, what wilt thou give me, seeing I go childless, and the steward of my house is this Eliezer of Damascus? And Abram said, Behold, to me thou hast given no seed: and, lo, one born in my house is mine heir.
>
> And, behold, the word of the LORD came unto him, saying, This shall not be thine heir; but he that shall come forth out of thine own bowels shall be thine heir. And he brought him forth abroad, and said, Look now toward heaven, and tell the stars, if thou be able to number them: and he said unto him, So shall thy seed be. <u>And he believed in the LORD; and he counted it to him for righteousness.</u> (Genesis 15:1 – 6)

It is upon this occasion that the LORD pronounces Abraham "righteous" on the basis of his faith alone, making him the pattern of all who put their trust in God. It is this event that Paul refers to in Roman 4:2 – 5 *For if Abraham were justified by works, he hath whereof to glory; but not before God. For what saith the Scripture? Abraham believed God, and it was counted* (reckoned / put on his account), *for righteousness. Now to him that worketh is the reward not reckoned of grace* (that is, not considered a gift), *but of debt* (that is, as something that was owed to him). *But to him that worketh not, but believeth on him that justified the ungodly, his faith is counted* (reckoned / put on his account) *for righteousness.* Thus Abraham forever bequeaths the blessing of demonstrating how grace works through our faith to bring us to a righteous standing before God.

And he said unto him, I am the LORD that brought thee out of Ur of the Chaldees, <u>to give thee this land to inherit it</u>. And he said, Lord GOD, whereby shall I know that I shall inherit it? And he said unto him, Take me an heifer of three years old, and a she goat of three years old, and a ram of three years old, and a turtledove, and a young pigeon. And he took unto him all these, and divided them in the midst, and laid each piece one against another: but the birds divided he not. And when the fowls came down upon the carcases, Abram drove them away. And when the sun was going down, a deep sleep fell upon Abram; and, lo, an horror of great darkness fell upon him.

*And he said unto Abram, Know of a surety that thy seed shall be a stranger in a land that is not theirs, and shall serve them; and they shall afflict them four hundred years; And also that nation, whom they shall serve, will I judge: and afterward shall they come out with great substance. And thou shalt go to thy fathers in peace; thou shalt be buried in a good old age. But in the fourth generation they shall come hither again: for the iniquity of the Amorites is not yet full. And it came to pass, that, when the sun went down, and it was dark, behold a smoking furnace, and a burning lamp that passed between those pieces. In the same day the LORD made a covenant with Abram, saying, Unto thy seed have I given this land**, <u>from the river of Egypt unto the great river, the river Euphrates</u>***: The Kenites, and the Kenizzites, and the Kadmonites, And the Hittites, and the Perizzites, and the Rephaims, And the Amorites, and the Canaanites, and the Girgashites, and the Jebusites (Genesis 15:7 – 21).*

In this passage God "cuts a covenant" with Abraham in which He alone passes between the pieces. In any kind of a reciprocal covenant, both of the covenant parties would pass between the pieces, each thus responsible to keep his part of the agreement. But here, only God passes through, thus it is evident that we are meant to understand that God is making Himself alone responsible for the fulfillment of the covenant made here. This then is very clearly an unconditional covenant resting in its totality upon the faithfulness and veracity of God.

Notice that while there is a prophetic element in this covenant, the terms of the covenant have not changed. God had made promises to Abraham, now He formalized those in the accepted customary fashion, and, as if that were not enough, he will later (Genesis 22:16) take an oath that the promises made and the covenant sealed will be performed. As the writer to Hebrews puts it, *When God made promise to Abraham, because he could swear by no greater, he sware by himself, Saying, Surely blessing I will bless thee, and multiplying I will multiply thee* (Hebrews 6:13, 14).

It is in this context that God describes the Land which He promised to Abraham's seed as, *From the river of Egypt, unto the great river, the river Euphrates;* and then enumerates the nations that were occupying that land at that time, all of which, in God's time, were to be dispossessed, *for the iniquity of the Amorites is not yet full.*

The reference to their "iniquity," is to the complete corruption that was then festering in Canaan that would eventually call for their utter destruction. The Canaanites were guilty of much the same sins that brought the Flood in the days of Noah and the destruction to Sodom and her sister cities in chapter nineteen. It is here in chapter fifteen that God ratifies the promises He made to Abraham earlier.

Chapter seventeen brings us to the next recorded instance where God reiterates His covenant and expands it. It is of particular importance because the emphasis here is on the perpetuity of the covenant. Note the words we have underlined in the text:

And when Abram was ninety years old and nine,
the LORD appeared to Abram, and said unto him,
I am the Almighty God; walk before me, and be
thou perfect. And I will make my covenant
between me and thee, and will multiply thee
exceedingly. And Abram fell on his face: and God
talked with him, saying, As for me, behold, my
covenant is with thee, and thou shalt be a father of
many nations. Neither shall thy name any more be
called Abram, but thy name shall be Abraham; for
a father of many nations have I made thee. And I
will make thee exceeding fruitful, and I will make
nations of thee, and kings shall come out of thee.
And I will establish my covenant between me and
thee and thy seed after thee in their generations
<u>for an everlasting covenant</u>, to be a God unto thee,
and to thy seed after thee. And I will give unto
thee, and to thy seed after thee, the land wherein
thou art a stranger, all the land of Canaan, <u>for an</u>
<u>everlasting possession</u>; and I will be their God
(Genesis 17:1 – 8).

This is then an "everlasting covenant" and an "everlasting possession" goes with it and it rests fully upon the ***I will*** of God, not the performance of either Abraham or his posterity.

The final time God reiterates the Covenant to Abraham is on the occasion of the sacrifice of his son Isaac in Genesis chapter twenty two. Note carefully the wording:

And the angel of the LORD called unto Abraham
out of heaven the second time, And said, <u>By myself</u>
<u>have I sworn, saith the LORD</u>, for because thou
hast done this thing, and hast not withheld thy son,
thine only son: That in blessing I will bless thee,
and in multiplying I will multiply thy seed as the
stars of the heaven, and as the sand which is upon
the sea shore; and thy seed shall possess the gate

of his enemies; <u>And in thy seed shall all the</u>
<u>nations of the earth be blessed</u>; because thou hast
obeyed my voice (Genesis 22:15 – 18).

It is here that God takes the oath, swearing by Himself that all He has promised and the covenant which He had sealed will be performed. There is no wiggle room here – God intended Abraham to know of a surety that what He had promised he would of Himself bring to pass.

Having looked then at the repeated and expanded Covenant which God made with Abraham, we will look next at the extension of the Abrahamic Covenant and its promises to Abraham's posterity.

The Extension of the Covenant to Abraham's Posterity

It is now important that we trace the continuance of the Covenant promises to Abraham's seed. In chapter twenty six we find God establishing the promises of the Abrahamic Covenant with Isaac. It is little wonder that Islam continues to attempt to perpetuate the fiction that Ishmael (not Isaac) was the son of promise, the son of the sacrifice and the builder of the Kaaba in Mecca. All of the promises of God concerning the Land are vouchsafed to Abraham's heir – which Scripture plainly identifies as Isaac, so the presence of Isaac as the heir invalidates all of Islam's fantasy.

Please remember that in choosing Isaac as the heir to the promise, God did not forget Ishmael or leave him destitute. There are two places where God made promises regarding Ishmael: first to his mother Hagar when she fled from her mistress Sarah, and second when Abraham pleaded that Ishmael might live before God. Both of them follow:

Then the Lord said, I will give you so many
descendants that no one will be able to count them.
You are going to have a son, and you will name him
Ishmael, because the LORD has heard your cry of
distress. But your son will live like a wild donkey;

he will be against everyone, and everyone will be
against him. He will live apart from all his relatives
(Genesis 16:10 – 12 GNB).

And as for Ishmael, I have heard thee: Behold, I
have blessed him, and will make him fruitful, and
will multiply him exceedingly; twelve princes shall
he beget, and I will make him a great nation
(Genesis 17:20, 21).

All God promised He did for Ishmael. There are twelve "Arab"
nations and the wealth and power they possess is beyond
calculation. The territory they occupy covers most of the Middle
East and all of North Africa. Ishmael has been abundantly blessed.
But God is careful to repeat again and again that His Covenant will
be with Isaac.

And the LORD appeared unto him (Isaac), *and*
said, Go not down into Egypt; dwell in the land
which I shall tell thee of: Sojourn in this land, and
I will be with thee, and will bless thee; for unto
thee, and unto thy seed, I will give all these
countries, and I will perform the oath which I
sware unto Abraham thy father; And I will make
thy seed to multiply as the stars of heaven, and
will give unto thy seed all these countries; and in
thy seed shall all the nations of the earth be
blessed(Genesis 26:2 – 5).

Further, after reiterating the covenant to Isaac, the Covenant
promises must now go to Isaac's heir – but God reverses the
natural order (Genesis 25:23). Esau was the older and therefore
the natural heir, but Jacob is chosen by God as the heir. Although
he actually secured his position by dubious and dishonest means,
God had determined His choice beforehand: *For the children being*
not yet born, neither having done any good or evil, that the
purpose of God according to election might stand, not of works,
but of him that calleth; it was said unto her, the elder shall serve
the younger (Roman 9:11, 12). Hence Jacob becomes the heir. So,

does the Covenant with Abraham extend to him as well? In Genesis chapter twenty eight we read:

> *And he dreamed, and behold a ladder set up on the earth, and the top of it reached to heaven: and behold the angels of God ascending and descending on it. And, behold, the LORD stood above it, and said, I am the LORD God of Abraham thy father, and the God of Isaac: the land whereon thou liest, to thee will I give it, and to thy seed; And thy seed shall be as the dust of the earth, and thou shalt spread abroad to the west, and to the east, and to the north, and to the south: and in thee and in thy seed shall all the families of the earth be blessed. And, behold, I am with thee, and will keep thee in all places whither thou goest, and will bring thee again into this land; for I will not leave thee, until I have done that which I have spoken to thee of* (Genesis 28:12 – 15).

Perhaps someone is tempted to ask, does the perpetuity of the promise terminate at some point? God anticipated that question and in Psalm one hundred and five He testifies:

> *He hath remembered his covenant forever, the word which he commanded to a thousand generations. Which covenant he made with Abraham, and his oath unto Isaac; And confirmed the same unto Jacob for a law, and to Israel for an everlasting covenant: Saying, Unto thee will I give the land of Canaan, the lot of your inheritance: When they were but a few men in number; yea, very few, and strangers in it* (Psalms 105:9 – 12).

A thousand generations is an expression that basically means, on into infinity or in other words, this Covenant never ends.

So to summarize, we have seen that Israel's future blessings rest entirely upon the unconditional covenants made with her

Patriarchs, and by extension with their descendents in perpetuity. As noted previously, the three aspects of this Covenant are enlarged and elaborated upon in the Palestinian Covenant, the Davidic Covenant and the New Covenant. Abraham is promised a Land, a Seed and a Blessing and within the fulfillment of these promises there is a host of eschatological ramifications.

As Dr. Dwight Pentecost says, "This covenant then (the Abrahamic), determines the whole future program for the nation Israel and is a major factor in Biblical Eschatology." 7

Chapter Two – The Land, The Seed and The Blessing

Since we are seeking to discover a rational for affirming Israel's future conversion, we have said that the first line of evidence can be traced to the covenants found in the OT. We have begun by looking at some of the promises covenanted to Israel by God. The foundational Covenant is of course the Abrahamic Covenant. As with the Abrahamic covenant, we will find that God is the initiator in each of these other covenants which grow out of the promises of the Abrahamic Covenant.

Since we are talking primarily about the covenanted conversion of Israel we will be focusing primarily upon that promise. However, before we leave the subject of these unconditional covenants which God initiated, we must at least briefly look at the provisions of the three covenants which have their roots in the Abrahamic Covenant, namely the Palestinian, the Davidic and the New Covenants. As we do so, we will find that each has, along with its own particular theme or emphasis, at least a subtle hint of the promise of spiritual conversion if not an outright statement concerning it.

The Palestinian Covenant

The terms of the Palestinian Covenant are found in a lengthy passage in the book of Deuteronomy chapter 29, 30. While in each former statement of this Covenant, the unconditional nature has been the emphasis, in this passage the emphasis is upon Israel's actual enjoyment of the Land Covenant, which is made conditioned upon her obedience to the Law.

Remember, that this passage comes four hundred and thirty years after God's unconditional promise to Abraham and now Israel has entered into another Covenant, the conditional Covenant of the Mosaic Law. The Law is a revelation of the perfect righteousness of God and is meant to govern every part of the Hebrew's life. This Covenant is completely conditional upon the obedience of the people to keep it, and hence the blessings under it are conditional as well.

It is well to remember however the words of the Holy Spirit as recorded in Galatians, *And this I say, that the covenant* (the Covenant with Abraham), *that was confirmed before of God in Christ, the law, which was four hundred and thirty years after, cannot disannul, that it should make the promise of none effect. For if the inheritance be of the law, it is no more of promise: but God gave it to Abraham by promise* (Galatians 3:17, 18).

The coming in of a Covenant of Law could not effect the validity of the promises made to Abraham, but it could, and did, condition the way those promises could be enjoyed. The passage in Deuteronomy clearly spells out the catastrophe of Israel's disobedience, but in the midst of that warning is the clear promise of restoration and conversion.

> *If any of thine be driven out unto the outmost parts of heaven, from thence will the LORD thy God gather thee, and from thence will he fetch thee: And the LORD thy God will bring thee into the land which thy fathers possessed, and thou shalt possess it; and he will do thee good, and multiply thee above thy fathers.* <u>*And the LORD thy God will circumcise thine heart, and the heart of thy seed, to love the LORD thy God with all thine heart, and with all thy soul, that thou mayest live.*</u>
> (Deuteronomy 30:4 – 6)

The idea of "circumcising the heart" is paramount to conversion. Sin is removed and the heart is rendered "new". It is a heart that loves and serves God, and that is the essence of conversion. Note

34

that this promise becomes a part of the Palestinian Covenant and is part and parcel with all of its other blessings.

Dr. Dwight Pentecost analyses Deuteronomy chapters twenty eight through thirty as follows:

> An analysis of this passage will show that there are seven main features in the program there unfolded: (1) The nation will be plucked off the land for its unfaithfulness (Deut. 28:63-68; 30:1-3) ; (2) there will be a future repentance of Israel (Deut. 28:63-68; 30: 1-3) ; (3) their Messiah will return (Deut. 30:3-6) ; (4) Israel will be restored to the land (Deut. 30:5) ; (5) Israel will be converted as a nation (Deut. 30:4-8; cf. Rom. 11:26-27) ; (6) Israel's enemies will be judged (Deut. 30:7); (7) the nation will then receive her full blessing (Deut. 30: 9). 8

While I might have put the above list in a slightly different order, Dr. Pentecost has clearly defined the content of the passage. Notice that while there is chastening for Israel and removal from the Land, there is also the absolute guarantee by God that there will come a spiritual conversion to Israel which will be followed by a complete restoration and the fulfillment of God's Covenant promises. Don't miss this!

No one who is knowledgeable and honest about the history of Israel can seriously argue that any such spiritual transformation has taken place even during the period after the captivities. As we will point out later, the curses of the Palestinian Covenant have all been fulfilled literally, why should we not expect the blessing to be fulfilled in the same way? We will see that Israel's covenanted conversion is the key to understanding the prophetic future.

In case anyone missed the point in chapter thirty, Moses makes it very clear in chapter thirty two that God has been looking after His chosen people from the beginning of creation and He will not forsake them now. Yes, they are disobedient, and yes, they have failed and will have to suffer the consequences of those failures, but God's purposes will not be frustrated by man's failures.

On a similar note, our Lord declared, *I will build my church and the gates of hell shall not prevail against it* (Matthew 16:18). Has the church not failed in its performance? Have we who are so highly privileged not disgraced that Holy Name by which we are called? Indeed, for shame, we have. But the dictum is still true: God's purposes will not be frustrated by man's failures; either with the Church or with Israel. The purposes and promises of God are yea and amen in Him.

> *He is the Rock, his work is perfect: for all his ways are judgment: a God of truth and without iniquity, just and right is he. They have corrupted themselves, their spot is not the spot of his children: they are a perverse and crooked generation. Do ye thus require the LORD, O foolish people and unwise? is not he thy father that hath bought thee? hath he not made thee, and established thee? Remember the days of old, consider the years of many generations: ask thy father, and he will shew thee; thy elders, and they will tell thee. When the most High divided to the nations their inheritance, when he separated the sons of Adam, he set the bounds of the people according to the number of the children of Israel. For the LORD'S portion is his people; Jacob is the lot of his inheritance. He found him in a desert land, and in the waste howling wilderness; he led him about, he instructed him, he kept him as the apple of his eye. As an eagle stirreth up her nest, fluttereth over her young, spreadeth abroad her wings, taketh them, beareth them on her wings: So the LORD alone did lead him, and there was no strange god with him* (Deuteronomy 32:4 – 12).

So we see that the Palestinian Covenant incorporates not only the unconditional promise of God that Israel, after long and tragic dispersal, will one day occupy the Land, but that she will be given a new heart and a new birth so that it can happen in a way that vindicates the righteousness of God. As we have said before, Israel's covenanted conversion is the key to understanding the prophetic future.

The Davidic Covenant

The Davidic Covenant concerns itself particularly with the "Seed" promises of the Abrahamic Covenant. God promised a seed to Abraham. We have already seen how that seed was to come through Isaac, the son of promise, and thence to Jacob by God's elective choice. Now the promise reemerges in the line of David and David's Seed.

> *Now therefore so shalt thou say unto my servant David, Thus saith the LORD of hosts, I took thee from the sheepcote, from following the sheep, to be ruler over my people, over Israel: And I was with thee whithersoever thou wentest, and have cut off all thine enemies out of thy sight, and have made thee a great name, like unto the name of the great men that are in the earth. <u>Moreover I will appoint a place for my people Israel, and will plant them, that they may dwell in a place of their own</u>, and move no more; neither shall the children of wickedness afflict them any more, as beforetime, And as since the time that I commanded judges to be over my people Israel, and have caused thee to rest from all thine enemies.*

> *Also the LORD telleth thee that he will make thee an house. And when thy days be fulfilled, and thou shalt sleep with thy fathers, <u>I will set up thy seed after thee, which shall proceed out of thy bowels,</u> and I will establish his kingdom. He shall build an house for my name, and <u>I will establish the throne of his kingdom for ever.</u> I will be his father, and he shall be my son. If he commit iniquity, I will*

chasten him with the rod of men, and with the stripes of the children of men: But my mercy shall not depart away from him, as I took it from Saul, whom I put away before thee. And thine house and thy kingdom shall be established for ever before thee: thy throne shall be established for ever (2 Samuel 7:8 – 16).

Notice that even here the Land which God promised to Israel is not, and cannot be separated from the promise. God promises both the perpetuity of David's Kingdom and the perpetuity of the Land to His people. As is common with prophecy, there is a double reference implied here. David's seed will be God's son, in the immediate sense through Solomon, and he will know the discipline of God along with the blessing. But David's greater Seed will be God's Son in the person of Jesus Christ and therefore David's dynasty will continue forever in the everlasting King who will sit upon David's throne.

There can be no doubt that that is exactly what the Angel is referencing when he declared to a young Jewish virgin, *And behold, thou shalt conceive in thy womb, and bring forth a son, and shalt call his name JESUS. He shall be great, and shall be called the Son of the Highest: and the Lord God shall give unto him the throne of his father David: And he shall reign over the house of Jacob for ever; and of his kingdom there shall be no end.* (Luke 1:31 – 33)

Thus, among other things, the Seed promise guarantees that the Messiah will be born and come of David's line (see Matthew 1:1 – 16), that He will be very God in the flesh, and that David's throne rights over the house of Jacob (Israel) will be vouchsafed to Him. Only a strange kind of exegetical alchemy can interpret this promise to mean anything but that Jesus will return and reign over Israel in the future, seated upon David's throne in Jerusalem from which David reigned.

Since it is evident that nothing of this has happened in the past it must be equally evident that what is promised here is destined to

38

be fulfilled in the future. Until now, the only crown Jesus Christ ever wore in Jerusalem was a crown of thorns. The fiction that Christ is presently on David's throne (when was David's throne ever in heaven) is a twisting of the plain words of Scripture. It must then be evident that these Old Testament Covenants, hold the key to understanding much of the prophetic future just before us.

We now have the assurance that in the future God will fulfill both the Land promises and the promises to the Seed of David (Christ). Further we have the promise that Israel's heart will be changed (circumcised / transformed) into one that will love and serve God. In all of this there is found the theme of a coming spiritual conversion for the nation.

But what about the promises of blessing? While there are many blessings involved in the other Covenants, the greatest of the "blessing" promises rests within the final Covenant – that which is called the New Covenant.

The New Covenant

The New Covenant is first revealed by Jeremiah in Chapter thirty one of his book.

> *Behold, the days come, saith the LORD, that I will make a new covenant with the house of Israel, and with the house of Judah: Not according to the covenant that I made with their fathers in the day that I took them by the hand to bring them out of the land of Egypt; which my covenant they brake, although I was an husband unto them, saith the LORD: But this shall be the covenant that I will make with the house of Israel; After those days, saith the LORD, I will put my law in their inward parts, and write it in their hearts; and will be their God, and they shall be my people. And they shall teach no more every man his neighbour, and every man his brother, saying, Know the LORD: for they*

shall all know me, from the least of them unto the greatest of them, saith the LORD: for I will forgive their iniquity, and I will remember their sin no more. Thus saith the LORD, which giveth the sun for a light by day, and the ordinances of the moon and of the stars for a light by night, which divideth the sea when the waves thereof roar; The LORD of hosts is his name: If those ordinances depart from before me, saith the LORD, then the seed of Israel also shall cease from being a nation before me for ever. Thus saith the LORD; If heaven above can be measured, and the foundations of the earth searched out beneath, I will also cast off all the seed of Israel for all that they have done, saith the LORD. (Jeremiah 31:31 – 37)

A careful analysis will reveal that the Covenant contains the following five guarantees:

1. It will be a Covenant distinctly different from the Mosaic Covenant (*that I made when I brought them out of Egypt*).
2. It will be an internalized covenant *written in their hearts*, not on stone.
3. It will be pervasive and national in scope, *for they shall all know me.*
4. It will accomplish the forgiveness of sins - *I will forgive their iniquity.*
5. It will insure that Israel as a nation will exist as long as time endures.

This Covenant was made with and vouchsafed to Israel (the nation), and it was this very Covenant that Jesus spoke of on the final night before His crucifixion when He said, *Take, eat; this is my body. And he took the cup, and gave thanks, and gave it to them, saying, Drink ye all of it; For this is my blood of the new testament (**diatheke**, i.e., New Covenant) which is shed for many for the remission of sins* (Matthew 26:26 – 28).

Remember, this ordinance was given first to Jewish men (Matthew 26:28; Mark 14:24; Luke 22:20), and grew out of the ordinance of the Passover. According to the usus loquendi, (the way the phrase would be used and understood in that time and location), those men, present around the table that night, would have understood Jesus to be talking about the same New Covenant predicted by Moses (Deuteronomy30:6) and described by Jeremiah (Jeremiah 31). There was no other "New Covenant" that they could have expected or been familiar with.

While the New Covenant was therefore not made with the Church, and its full promised blessings will not be fulfilled until the time of Israel's conversion, the spiritual blessings of the Covenant are available now because the Covenant was inaugurated by the death of the Covenant Maker. The Church (we who believe in this age, either Jew or Gentile), is brought into the blessings of the Covenant through a faith relationship to the Mediator of the Covenant; that is, to Christ!

This is the whole thrust of Galatians; *And the scripture, foreseeing that God would justify the heathen* (Gentiles) *through faith, preached before the gospel unto Abraham, saying, In thee shall all nations be blessed. So then they which be of faith are blessed with faithful Abraham. . . That the blessing of Abraham might come on the Gentiles through Jesus Christ; that we might receive the promise of the Spirit through faith. . . And if ye be Christ's, then are ye Abraham's seed, and heirs according to the promise.* (Galatians 3:8, 9, 14, 29)

The New Covenant is basically an extension of the third part of the Abrahamic Covenant, *"in thy Seed shall all the nations of the earth be blessed."* Abraham received that Covenant promise by faith. Scripture make clear that Christ is the Seed specifically promised to Abraham. Hence through faith in Christ, we enter into Abraham's blessing and become his spiritual children. And note: not by the Law, but by faith; *that the blessing of Abraham might come upon the Gentiles through Jesus Christ; that we might receive the promise of the Spirit* (it is that heart change produced by the Holy Spirit which the New Covenant promises) *through faith.*

Jesus' death laid the basis both for our salvation, and for the promised fulfillment of the New Covenant with Israel. The entire New Covenant promise is repeated in the book of Hebrews to prove the writers point that the old covenant of the Law was now replaced with a better covenant ratified in the blood of a better Sacrifice. He concludes the contrast between the old covenant and the new with these words, *In that he saith, A new covenant, he hath made the first old. Now that which decayeth and waxeth old is ready to vanish away.* (Hebrews 8:6 – 13)

"On the day of Christ's crucifixion the fountain was opened *potentially* for all Israel and the whole world. At the Second Advent of Christ, the fountain will be opened *experientially* for the Jewish nation. This spiritual cleansing of the nation is associated in other passages of Scripture with Israel's spiritual regeneration and the inauguration of the New Covenant." 9

So the Church comes into the blessing and benefit of the New Covenant through its faith relationship to the Covenant Maker and we now partake in the forgiveness of sins, the renewal of our hearts, and a personal relationship with the Lord Himself. But all of that does not mean that the exact terms of the Covenant will not be fulfilled with Israel. No, His death purchases both our redemption and the ultimate redemption of Israel as a nation.

SUMMARY:
Thus as we have reviewed the great unconditional covenants made with Israel. We have seen that Israel is promised a Land (the land their fathers possessed), a seed, not only of a multitude of decedents as numerous as the sand of the sea and the stars, but a specific Seed that would make the fulfillment of every other promise possible, and the blessing of a spiritual renewal that would make them a new people with a new heart.

Bishop J.C. Ryle, whom Spurgeon called, "the best man in the Church of England," summed it up well:

> It is high time for Christians to interpret unfulfilled prophecy by the light of prophecies already fulfilled. The curses of the Jews were brought to pass literally: so also will be the blessings. The scattering was literal: so also will be the gathering. The pulling down of Zion was literal: so also will be the building up. The rejection of Israel was literal: so also will be the restoration. I believe that the Jews shall ultimately be gathered again as a separate nation, restored to their own land, and converted to the faith of Christ, after going through great tribulation." 10

Bishop Ryle's remarks take on added significance when we recognize that they were written in the 1800s before any of the events of the last century took place. It was generally thought impossible for Israel to have been reconstituted a nation in her own land even one hundred years ago. Ryle's conclusions are therefore entirely based upon Scripture and not on current events.

In the next chapter we will begin to look at other passages that provide assurances of Israel's conversion, specifically the key passages found in the Old Testament prophets. They speak with a concerted voice.

Chapter Three: The Concerted Voice of the Prophets

We have seen that the four great eschatological covenants promise Israel a bright and glorious future despite her present condition of unbelief and enmity toward the gospel and the Savior Himself. The New Covenant in particular promises that all of that will change and Israel will be given a "new heart" that will love God and obey Him. In other words, it promises that Israel will be converted.

The element of conversion we noted was also present in the promises of the Palestinian Covenant, leading to the conclusion that there is a connection between Israel's conversion and her presence in the Land.

Now we turn to the voice of the prophets to learn what they have said on the matter, and we will find their words remarkably consistent and unanimous – they speak with a single voice. It will be our purpose in this section to let the prophets speak for themselves. We will have little need to say much by way of comment. Their own words will provide ample evidence.

ISAIAH

We will begin by looking at the prophet Isaiah. As you read the words, ask yourself, have the promises made here ever been fulfilled? If the answer is "no", then by the very nature and character of God we may be sure that they will be fulfilled in the future. We begin in Chapter one.

And I will turn my hand upon thee, and purely purge away thy dross, and take away all thy tin: And I will restore thy judges as at the first, and thy counsellors as at the beginning: afterward thou shalt be called, The city of righteousness, the faithful city. Zion shall be redeemed with judgment, and her converts with righteousness. (Isaiah 1:25 – 27)

Chapters eleven and twelve are replete with pictures of a restored and redeemed Israel. There are an abundance of predictions here that have never been fulfilled and therefore await future fulfillment. Chapter twelve is especially potent:

And in that day thou shalt say, O LORD, I will praise thee: though thou wast angry with me, thine anger is turned away, and thou comfortedst me. Behold, God is my salvation; I will trust, and not be afraid: for the LORD JEHOVAH is my strength and my song; he also is become my salvation. Therefore with joy shall ye draw water out of the wells of salvation. And in that day shall ye say, Praise the LORD, call upon his name, declare his doings among the people, make mention that his name is exalted. Sing unto the LORD; for he hath done excellent things: this is known in all the earth. Cry out and shout, thou inhabitant of Zion: for great is the Holy One of Israel in the midst of thee. (Isaiah 12:1 –6)

Note in this passage, not only will Israel come to draw water out of the wells of salvation for themselves, but they will *Declare His name among the people,* that is, they will proclaim to all what God has done. The absolute assurance of God's words are proclaimed in Isaiah 14:24: *The LORD of hosts hath sworn, saying, Surely as I have thought, so shall it come to pass; and as I have purposed, so shall it stand.* In simple words, nothing will stand in the way of God's purpose or His plans.

Although Isaiah does not speak expressly of Israel's conversion in some of his prophecies, the prophet is consistent in proclaiming Israel's future restoration and glory. Chapters twenty four through twenty seven are full of that theme.

Chapters thirty two through thirty five take up the theme of the last days and God's gracious intervention bringing Israel together again in a safe resting place. In these chapters, Isaiah looks through the troubles of the Tribulation to the glories of the Kingdom age and Israel is the center of his predictions.

In chapters forty through forty six Jehovah challenges Israel about their lack of loyalty to Him comparing His infinite power to the impotency of idols. Mingled within the text are references to Israel's redemption;

> *I, even I, am he that blotteth out thy transgressions for mine own sake, and will not remember thy sins.* (Isaiah 43:25)

We in the Church Age may embrace that verse and take it to ourselves by application, but it's meaning within its context is the forgiveness and redemption of Israel.

> *Thus saith the LORD the King of Israel, and his redeemer the LORD of hosts; I am the first, and I am the last; and beside me there is no God . . . Remember these, O Jacob and Israel; for thou art my servant: I have formed thee; thou art my servant: O Israel, thou shalt not be forgotten of me. I have blotted out, as a thick cloud, thy transgressions, and, as a cloud, thy sins: return unto me; for I have redeemed thee. Sing, O ye heavens; for the LORD hath done it: shout, ye lower parts of the earth: break forth into singing, ye mountains, O forest, and every tree therein: for the LORD hath redeemed Jacob, and glorified himself in Israel. Thus saith the LORD, thy redeemer, and he that formed thee from the womb,*

I am the LORD that maketh all things; that stretcheth forth the heavens alone; that spreadeth abroad the earth by myself . . . That confirmeth the word of his servant, and performeth the counsel of his messengers; that saith to Jerusalem, Thou shalt be inhabited; and to the cities of Judah, Ye shall be built, and I will raise up the decayed places thereof. (Isaiah 44: 6, 21 – 26)

Hearken unto me, O house of Jacob, and all the remnant of the house of Israel, which are borne by me from the belly, which are carried from the womb: And even to your old age I am he; and even to hoar hairs will I carry you: I have made, and I will bear; even I will carry, and will deliver you (Isaiah 46:3, 4).

More specifically Jehovah declares that Israel will not only be redeemed, but will be a witness to the entire earth.

Therefore my people shall know my name: therefore they shall know in that day that I am he that doth speak: behold, it is I. How beautiful upon the mountains are the feet of him that bringeth good tidings, that publisheth peace; that bringeth good tidings of good, that publisheth salvation; that saith unto Zion, Thy God reigneth! Thy watchmen shall lift up the voice; with the voice together shall they sing: for they shall see eye to eye, when the LORD shall bring again Zion. Break forth into joy, sing together, ye waste places of Jerusalem: for the LORD hath comforted his people, he hath redeemed Jerusalem. The LORD hath made bare his holy arm in the eyes of all the nations; and all the ends of the earth shall see the salvation of our God. (Isaiah 52:6 – 10)

In chapter fifty four, Isaiah sees Israel as a rejected wife that has been restored. It is a beautiful chapter, full of hope and promise and is the same theme that is picked up later by the prophets, Jeremiah, Ezekiel and Hosea.

One final passage is found in chapter sixty six. Read this passage very carefully for we will consider it again as we examine the events surrounding Israel's conversion.

> *Before she travailed, she brought forth; before her pain came, she was delivered of a man child.*(Messiah, Jesus) *Who hath heard such a thing? who hath seen such things? Shall the earth be made to bring forth in one day? or shall a nation be born at once? for as soon as Zion travailed,*(in the time of Tribulation) *she brought forth her children. Shall I bring to the birth, and not cause to bring forth? saith the LORD: shall I cause to bring forth, and shut the womb? saith thy God. Rejoice ye with Jerusalem, and be glad with her, all ye that love her: rejoice for joy with her, all ye that mourn for her* (Isaiah 66:7 – 10).

Thus there is a constant thread of promise in Isaiah for Israel's restoration and conversion.

JEREMIAH

We turn now to the testimony of Jeremiah. One of the earliest promises of Israel's restoration is found in Jeremiah twenty three. Notice as you read the words, the connection between Israel's restoration and her redemption.

> *Behold, the days come, saith the LORD, that I will raise unto David a righteous Branch, and a King shall reign and prosper, and shall execute judgment and justice in the earth. In his days Judah shall be saved, and Israel shall dwell safely: and this is his name whereby he shall be called, THE LORD OUR RIGHTEOUSNESS. Therefore, behold, the days come, saith the LORD, that they shall no more say, The LORD liveth,*

which brought up the children of Israel out of the land of Egypt; But, The LORD liveth, which brought up and which led the seed of the house of Israel out of the north country, and from all countries whither I had driven them; and they shall dwell in their own land. (Jeremiah 23:5 – 8)

We have already looked at the New Covenant found in Jeremiah thirty one. Let's look again at just the part of that Covenant which particularly promises Israel's conversion;

After those days, saith the LORD, I will put my law in their inward parts, and write it in their hearts; and will be their God, and they shall be my people. And they shall teach no more every man his neighbour, and every man his brother, saying, Know the LORD: for they shall all know me, from the least of them unto the greatest of them, saith the LORD: for I will forgive their iniquity, and I will remember their sin no more. (Jeremiah 31:33, 34)

Jeremiah continues along the same vein in Chapter thirty two:

Behold, I will gather them out of all countries, whither I have driven them in mine anger, and in my fury, and in great wrath; and I will bring them again unto this place, and I will cause them to dwell safely: And they shall be my people, and I will be their God: And I will give them one heart, and one way, that they may fear me for ever, for the good of them, and of their children after them: And I will make an everlasting covenant with them, that I will not turn away from them, to do them good; but I will put my fear in their hearts, that they shall not depart from me. Yea, I will rejoice over them to do them good, and I will plant them in this land assuredly with my whole heart and with my whole soul. For thus saith the LORD;

> *Like as I have brought all this great evil upon this people, so will I bring upon them all the good that I have promised them.* (Jeremiah 32:37 – 42)

Another great promise is found in the very next chapter, chapter thirty three;

> *In those days, and at that time, will I cause the Branch of righteousness to grow up unto David; and he shall execute judgment and righteousness in the land. In those days shall Judah be saved, and Jerusalem shall dwell safely: and this is the name wherewith she shall be called, The LORD our righteousness.* (Jeremiah 33:15, 16)

In this passage again Jeremiah ties Israel's restoration and conversion to Messiah who is *The LORD our righteousness.*

EZEKIEL

Ezekiel is a prophet in exile with many others bearing the suffering that the nation's sins have brought upon them. Nevertheless he has a clear vision of a future for the nation. God promises the restoration of Israel and their ultimate conversion in these words:

> *I will even gather you from the people, and assemble you out of the countries where ye have been scattered, and I will give you the land of Israel. And they shall come thither, and they shall take away all the detestable things thereof and all the abominations thereof from thence. And I will give them one heart, and I will put a new spirit within you; and I will take the stony heart out of their flesh, and will give them an heart of flesh: That they may walk in my statutes, and keep mine ordinances, and do them: and they shall be my people, and I will be their God.* (Ezekiel 11:17 – 20)

Ezekiel's next mention of Israel's future conversion is found in chapter sixteen amidst Jehovah's rebuke to the nation for all her sinful ways.

> *Nevertheless I will remember my covenant with thee in the days of thy youth, and I will establish unto thee an everlasting covenant. Then thou shalt remember thy ways, and be ashamed, when thou shalt receive thy sisters, thine elder and thy younger: and I will give them unto thee for daughters, but not by thy covenant. And I will establish my covenant with thee; and thou shalt know that I am the LORD: That thou mayest remember, and be confounded, and never open thy mouth any more because of thy shame, when I am pacified toward thee for all that thou hast done, saith the Lord GOD.* (Ezekiel 16:60 – 63)

In chapter thirty four, Ezekiel pictures Israel as a flock that has been ill served of its shepherds. Then, beginning in verse eleven, Ezekiel pictures that flock being regathered and brought into a place of blessing. He sees David once more leading the people (an obvious reference to the Kingdom), and Israel "knowing the LORD their God."

> *. . . and they shall be safe in their land, and shall know that I am the LORD, when I have broken the bands of their yoke, and delivered them out of the hand of those that served themselves of them. And they shall no more be a prey to the heathen, neither shall the beast of the land devour them; but they shall dwell safely, and none shall make them afraid. And I will raise up for them a plant of renown, and they shall be no more consumed with hunger in the land, neither bear the shame of the heathen any more. Thus shall they know that I the LORD their God am with them, and that they, even the house of Israel, are my people, saith the Lord GOD. And ye my flock, the flock of my pasture, are*

men, and I am your God, saith the Lord GOD.
(Ezekiel 34:27 – 31)

The heart of Ezekiel's prophecy of Israel's conversion is contained in chapters thirty six through thirty nine. The passage is too long to look at here and will be examined more closely when we look at the circumstances that will surround and lead up to that event. But the key verses of chapter thirty six are pertinent here:

> *For I will take you from among the heathen, and gather you out of all countries, and will bring you into your own land. Then will I sprinkle clean water upon you, and ye shall be clean: from all your filthiness, and from all your idols, will I cleanse you. A new heart also will I give you, and a new spirit will I put within you: and I will take away the stony heart out of your flesh, and I will give you an heart of flesh. And I will put my spirit within you, and cause you to walk in my statutes, and ye shall keep my judgments, and do them. And ye shall dwell in the land that I gave to your fathers; and ye shall be my people, and I will be your God.* (Ezekiel 36:24 – 28)

In perfect concert with the testimony of all the former prophets, Ezekiel affirms the fact that Israel has a future and that her future involves a complete restoration and conversion of heart to Jehovah God.

DANIEL

The prophet Daniel had a most unusual ministry. He was a Jewish prophet to a Gentile court. While Daniel is full of prophecies about future events, those events pertain primarily to the Gentile nations to whom he prophesied. However, Daniel loved his nation and prayed earnestly for their future and was permitted to prophecy the exact time of the coming of Messiah, His subsequent death, the desolations of Jerusalem that occurred in 70 AD and the time of trouble known as Daniel's seventieth week which we know best as the Great Tribulation.

But while all these events certainly concerned and touch the people of Israel, Daniel had a deep desire to see their final days and he was permitted to do so in few verses in the final chapter of his book.

> *And at that time shall Michael stand up, the great prince which standeth for the children of thy people: and there shall be a time of trouble, such as never was since there was a nation even to that same time: and at that time thy people shall be delivered, every one that shall be found written in the book. And many of them that sleep in the dust of the earth shall awake, some to everlasting life, and some to shame and everlasting contempt. And they that be wise shall shine as the brightness of the firmament; and they that turn many to righteousness as the stars for ever and ever.*
> (Daniel 12:1 –3)

So in just a few verses, Daniel is allowed to take us from the beginning to the end of the Tribulation period. Notice there will be at that time a people, *that shall be found written in the book.* In other words, Daniel predicts a converted multitude. Notice too that they are Daniel's people, that is, the Jewish nation. Finally, do not miss the fact that they will do exploits for God by turning many to righteousness. That point will be important later on in our study.

HOSEA

To understand the prophecies of Hosea, it is necessary to understand the peculiar ministry assigned to the prophet. Hosea was not only a preaching prophet, but a sign to Israel that reflected the nation itself. He was instructed to *take unto thee a wife of whoredoms and children of whoredoms* (Hosea 1:2), an assignment he obeyed in taking Gomer as his wife. While some commentators shrink from accepting that God actually assigned His prophet such a task, I see no way of justifying any other interpretation.

In doing what he did, Hosea's relationship to his adulterous wife became a living sign or parable of God's relationship to adulterous Israel. He had "married them by covenant" at Sinai, and they had consistently been unfaithful to their Covenant vows.

Hosea's wife bore three children. The first was a son Hosea named Jezreel. Like Isaiah before him he could say, *Behold I and the children that the LORD hath given me are for signs and for wonders in Israel* (Isaiah 8:18). Careful reading of the text would suggest that the next two children did not belong to Hosea but were conceived in adultery.

The first Hosea names Lo-ruhamah which translates roughly as "not loved or pitied." It would be very unlikely that a father would say that about his own child. The final child seems clearly to be born of fornication and is named, Lo-Ammi, which means, "not my people." All of this is used of God as a sign to Israel of their own unfaithfulness to Him.

Finally, in chapter two, Hosea pronounces the words, *Plead with your mother, Plead: for she is not my wife, neither am I her husband:* (Hosea 2:2). The words are the ancient formula for divorce. While there is every evidence that despite her profligate ways, Hosea had learned to love his wife, he is left with no choice now but to separate himself from her.

There are several similar passages in the prophets all of which play upon this same theme of Israel being the unfaithful "wife of Jehovah" and the consequences of that. I suggest you read Isaiah 54:6, 7; Jeremiah 3:1-14, 20; Ezekiel 16:1 – 63; 23:1-49.

After Hosea divorces his wife however, her continuing conduct took her to a state of bondage. It is then that he is told to, *Go yet, love a woman beloved of her friend, yet an adulteress, according to the love of the LORD toward the children of Israel, who look to other gods, and love flagons of wine. So I bought her to me for fifteen pieces of silver, and for an homer of barley, and an half homer of barley* (Hosea 3:1, 2).

Her "price" was that of a female slave which was considered of little value. She is, however valuable to her former husband and he will now "betroth her to himself" once again. By the way, this is clear evidence that a divorce had indeed taken place – you do not betroth one to whom you are already married.

However, having purchased Gomer from her terrible condition, and betrothed her to himself, she is not allowed to see him but must "wait for him many days." Once again the drama of Israel's chequered career is acted out. But the ultimate goal is complete reconciliation and so Hosea says;

> *For the children of Israel shall abide many days without a king, and without a prince, and without a sacrifice, and without an image, and without an ephod, and without teraphim: Afterward shall the children of Israel return, and seek the LORD their God, and David their king; and shall fear the LORD and his goodness in the latter days.* (Hosea 3:4, 5)

In other words, Israel shall be without the true God and she shall be without idols or false gods as well. Israel will be desolate during the time of her waiting. And so she has been now for many centuries. The price of her redemption has been paid, but she is still separated from Jehovah, her Husband.

So as Hosea predicts Israel's final conversion and reconciliation with Jehovah, he gives her God's instructions about approaching Him. Those are found in the concluding verses of the book:

> *Take with you words, and turn to the LORD: say unto him, Take away all iniquity, and receive us graciously: so will we render the calves of our lips. Asshur(Assyria), shall not save us; we will not ride upon horses: neither will we say any more to the work of our hands, Ye are our gods: for in thee the fatherless findeth mercy.* (Hosea 14:2, 3)

Jehovah's gracious response is found in the final verses. It must be abundantly evident to any thinking person that the prediction and promise of this final verse has never yet been fulfilled. It is, therefore, in Israel's future.

> *I will heal their backsliding, I will love them*
> *freely: for mine anger is turned away from him.*
> *(Hosea 14:4)*

JOEL

Joel's prophecy is one that we shall return to later for a more specific examination, but the indications of his expectation of a dramatic conversion of the nation Israel are evident in these following familiar words. Please remember that while Peter used them to clarify what was happening on the day of Pentecost, it was the prophetic spiritual dynamics of the Feast that were being fulfilled on that day and not this specific prophecy. There were no *wonders in the heavens* nor *blood, and fire, and pillars of smoke,* on the Day of Pentecost. The sun did not turn into darkness or the moon into blood and the Day of the LORD did not commence at that time.

No, while the passage did help Peter's hearers understand that what was happening was a pouring out of God's Spirit upon the hearers, the fulfillment of this prediction waits another day when all of the natural phenomenon listed in the verse will indeed take place. Israel, as a nation (note the context) will experience it.

> *And it shall come to pass afterward, that I will*
> *pour out my spirit upon all flesh; and your sons*
> *and your daughters shall prophesy, your old men*
> *shall dream dreams, your young men shall see*
> *visions: And also upon the servants and upon the*
> *handmaids in those days will I pour out my spirit.*
> *And I will shew wonders in the heavens and in the*
> *earth, blood, and fire, and pillars of smoke. The*
> *sun shall be turned into darkness, and the moon*
> *into blood, before the great and the terrible day of*
> *the LORD come. And it shall come to pass, that*

whosoever shall call on the name of the LORD shall be delivered: for in mount Zion and in Jerusalem shall be deliverance, as the LORD hath said, and in the remnant whom the LORD shall call. (Joel 2:28 – 32)

The remainder of Joel's prophecy, found in chapter three, takes us to the final battle when all of the nations come against Israel. That subject is for another discussion.

AMOS

The prophesies of Amos are primarily focused on God's righteous judgments against both Israel and the surrounding nations. While he does not speak directly to Israel's conversion, he does have this to say about their final restoration:

In that day will I raise up the tabernacle of David that is fallen, and close up the breaches thereof; and I will raise up his ruins, and I will build it as in the days of old: That they may possess the remnant of Edom, and of all the heathen, which are called by my name, saith the LORD that doeth this. Behold, the days come, saith the LORD, that the plowman shall overtake the reaper, and the treader of grapes him that soweth seed; and the mountains shall drop sweet wine, and all the hills shall melt. And I will bring again the captivity of my people of Israel, and they shall build the waste cities, and inhabit them; and they shall plant vineyards, and drink the wine thereof; they shall also make gardens, and eat the fruit of them. And I will plant them upon their land, and they shall no more be pulled up out of their land which I have given them, saith the LORD thy God. (Amos 9:11 – 15)

It should be noted that reference is made to this verse by the Apostles at the Jerusalem Council (Acts 15:13 – 17). After Peter (Simeon), had declared how God had begun to take out from among the Gentiles a people for His name, James recalls this passage. Note that he says, "after this," that is, "after God has taken a people from among the Gentiles, then he will build again the tabernacle of David, etc." Today, God is still taking out a people for His own name from the nations, but when the Church is complete, He will again turn His attention to restoring Israel as He clearly indicates here.

MICAH

Once again the prophet Micah does not speak directly of the event of Israel's conversion, but rather he describes vividly the results of both her restoration and her conversion. Israel will teach the world to "know the LORD". How marvelous is that?

> *But in the last days it shall come to pass, that the mountain of the house of the LORD shall be established in the top of the mountains, and it shall be exalted above the hills; and people shall flow unto it. And many nations shall come, and say, Come, and let us go up to the mountain of the LORD, and to the house of the God of Jacob; and he will teach us of his ways, and we will walk in his paths: for the law shall go forth of Zion, and the word of the LORD from Jerusalem. And he shall judge among many people, and rebuke strong nations afar off; and they shall beat their swords into plowshares, and their spears into pruninghooks: nation shall not lift up a sword against nation, neither shall they learn war any more. But they shall sit every man under his vine and under his fig tree; and none shall make them afraid: for the mouth of the LORD of hosts hath spoken it. For all people will walk every one in the name of his god, and we will walk in the name of the LORD our God for ever and ever. In that day, saith the LORD, will I assemble her that halteth, and I will gather her that is driven out, and her that I have afflicted; And I will make her that halted a remnant, and her that was cast far off a*

strong nation: and the LORD shall reign over them in mount Zion from henceforth, even for ever. (Micah 4:1-7)

In chapter seven, Micah prophesies of a time when God will pardon Israel and take away their sins. By any measurement, that is spiritual conversion.

Who is a God like unto thee, that pardoneth iniquity, and passeth by the transgression of the remnant of his heritage? he retaineth not his anger for ever, because he delighteth in mercy. He will turn again, he will have compassion upon us; he will subdue our iniquities; and thou wilt cast all their sins into the depths of the sea. Thou wilt perform the truth to Jacob, and the mercy to Abraham, which thou hast sworn unto our fathers from the days of old. (Micah 7:18 – 20)

ZECHARIAH

While most of the remaining prophets make a number of prophetic statements concerning end time events, there seems to be no direct reference to a moment of conversion for Israel except perhaps this one in Zechariah.

And I will pour upon the house of David, and upon the inhabitants of Jerusalem, the spirit of grace and of supplications: and they shall look upon me whom they have pierced, and they shall mourn for him, as one mourneth for his only son, and shall be in bitterness for him, as one that is in bitterness for his firstborn. (Zechariah 12:10)

While this experience may come later in the actual drama of Israel's conversion, it is a clear declaration that a spiritual conversion will occur. Taken together the voice of the prophets is unanimous and unequivocal – God has determined to bring His Covenant people out of their stubborn unbelief to a humble repentance and awakening that will result in a new spirit (the Holy

Spirit), and a new heart. That is the clear teaching of the Old Testament Scriptures.

But what of the New Testament? Is there any assurance of Israel's future conversion there, or has the Church now replaced Israel forever? Paul answers that question just as unequivocally as the Old Testament prophets did. We refer to the ninth, tenth and eleventh chapters of St. Paul's Epistle to the Romans.

Chapter Four: The New Testament Speaks – Romans 9 – 11

The Epistle of Paul to the Romans is very possibly the most important book theologically in the New Testament. The person that has a proper grasp of the teaching of the book of Romans will be sound in the Faith at every point. Romans is possibly the most difficult and extensive treatise in the Bible. Paul seemed determined, when writing to those who found themselves in the most important city of that time, to address every question, answer every objection, confront every problem and expound every aspect of Christ's doctrine and life. Romans is the only treatise in all the writings of the world where a satisfying and logical rational is set forth for man as he is and things as they are.

Without a doubt, the most contested and hotly debated passage of prophetic Scripture in the New Testament Epistles is contained in the three chapters, 9, 10 and 11 of Romans. This is not because the passage is particularly difficult to understand if it is allowed to "speak for itself" in a literal / historical / grammatical sense. It is rather because, when understood in that way, it contradicts the assumptions of those who believe that the natural seed of Abraham, the Jewish people, have been forever rejected and that the New Testament Church has now superseded ethnic Israel and is heir to all the promises made to her in the Scriptures. While this Replacement Theology admits to the conversion of individual Jewish people, it can concede no future conversion of the nation, or a future restoration of National Israel. It therefore admits of no future millennial reign of Christ on a literal "Throne of David."

In his excellent book, *Future Israel*, author Barry E. Horner states his own conclusions and conviction concerning Israel's future especially as it is found in the Romans passage. It should be noted that Horner is a Reformed Theologian and therefore his conclusions come with even more force in a day when Reformed Theology has become automatically equated with Amillennialism and Replacement Theology. Horner states:

> "Even among Christians of this twentieth century who are indebted to the Reformation for the recovery of the gospel of the free grace of God, there has been vigorous disagreement with regard to the future destiny of Israel. My own strong commitment is to God's eschatological promise of a regenerated nation of Israel in the land under its acknowledged Messiah, the Lord Jesus Christ. I believe that a *prima facie* reading of Romans 9-11 readily leads to this conclusion and that only a preconceived, dominant system of doctrine such as that of the Roman Catholic Church, or of entrenched Augustinianism, forces an alternative interpretation." 11

We will attempt to examine in some detail what is contained in these chapters from, as Horner puts it, "a *prima facie* reading of Romans 9-11." I have attempted to outline the general flow of Paul's arguments.

Israel's Past: Chosen In Electing Grace: Romans 9:1 –29

- **Paul's Passion 9:1-3**

It hard to imagine how Paul could have used stronger language that that which we find here. His deep love for the people of Israel and concern for them goes beyond anything most of us can imagine. Listen to his words; *I could wish that myself were accursed from Christ for my brethren, my kinsmen according to the flesh:"* Only Moses comes near the equal when, after Israel had replaced Jehovah with a Golden Calf he pleaded with God for them in these words; *Yet now, if thou wilt forgive their sin--; and if not, blot me,*

I pray thee, out of thy book which thou hast written. (Exodus 32:32)

Both men exhibit that unfathomable compassion that is the nature of God. It is only when we know that kind of compassion that we can reasonably understand what Paul is going to argue here. In spite of all her terrible failures, and in spite of the hardness she demonstrates to this day, God has a future for Israel and He will restore her once again to Himself. Let's follow as Paul develops that theme.

- **Jewish Privilege 9:4,5**

In these next two verses, Paul sets forth something of the remarkable privileges which God had bestowed on Israel in these words, *Who are Israelites; to whom pertaineth the adoption, and the glory, and the covenants, and the giving of the law, and the service of God, and the promises; Whose are the fathers, and of whom as concerning the flesh Christ came, who is over all, God blessed for ever. Amen.* Look at the privilege – they are chosen of God and brought into His family – God called Israel alone of the nations "my son" (Exodus 4:22; Hosea 11:1), and it is with them that God established His covenants. It is reflective of just how important the covenants are in God's relationship to Israel that Paul refers to them here. They were given the Law (compare Romans 2:17 – 19), and the promises, and the Patriarchs belong to them. God delights to be known as "the God of Abraham, Isaac and Jacob" (Matthew 22:32). Finally, it is of Israel that Christ came – how great a privilege is that? So Paul's point is, Israel is a very privileged people.

Before you leave this however, don't miss the obvious declaration of Christ's Deity here. It is a little obscure in the KJV, but the BBE translates it, *and of whom came Christ in the flesh, who is over all, God, to whom be blessing for ever.* Yes, Jesus is God!

- **Not all Israel is Israel 9:6 – 13**

In these verses Paul seeks to make a distinction between those who were simply the physical descendants of the family of Abraham and those who are spiritual children through faith. The argument is that there have always been (as early as Ishmael and Isaac) those who were only natural descendents and those who are chosen, elect and in relationship to God.

C. I. Scofield explains; "The distinction is between Israel after the flesh, the mere natural posterity of Abraham, and Israelites who, through faith, are also Abraham's spiritual children. Gentiles who believe are also of Abraham's spiritual seed; but here the apostle is not considering them, but only the two kinds of Israelites, the natural and the spiritual Israel." 12

Paul next demonstrates this principle by two very relevant historic illustrations. First he reminds us that, although Abraham had a son by Hagar, God rejected him from the place of privilege and chose Isaac, the son of promise. Please do not read into this the idea of eternal salvation or damnation. That is not the consideration. The point in both these examples is God's elective choice of the one He will favor to bear the covenant promise, *"in thy seed shall all the nations of the earth be blessed."* So God chose Isaac over Ishmael.

But lest anyone say that God's choice was based on human factors (i.e., Ishmael was the son of a handmaid), Paul next moves to the case of Esau and Jacob. These boys were twins. Born of the same parents and at the same time, except that in the natural order of things, Esau, who came out first, would have inherited the blessings. But God chose Jacob, when the children had done neither good or evil – proving that His choice rests, not upon merit or performance, but upon God's unfathomable grace.

We must not leave this section however, without at least looking at verse 13. *As it is written, Jacob have I loved, but Esau have I hated.* Note that this quote was not spoken as the former was, before the children were born or had done good or evil. This quote is taken from the last book of the Old Testament (Malachi 1:2, 3), and is spoken in the context of God reminding his people how much God had loved them and done for them, so as by contrast it could be said, *Jacob have I loved, but Esau have I hated.* Once again, the issue is not eternal life, and nothing in these passages can be construed, as some have done, to teach that God predestines some to heaven and others to hell. Paul's point is that there have always been a part of Israel who were simply Israelites by natural birth, and there have been others who have been chosen to have a part in the covenant promises of God.

- **The Mercy and Justice of God 9:14 – 24**

Paul argument continues with the implied question, Is God unrighteous? In our vernacular, we would have said, "Is God fair" perhaps even implying that He is not. Paul responds again by referring to God's response to Moses at the time that all Israel had made and worshipped a golden calf at the very moment God was delivering His perfect Law to Moses. They deserved to be destroyed, but God elected to exercise His Sovereign right to show mercy; *I will have mercy on whom I will have mercy, and I will have compassion on whom I will have compassion.* (Romans 9:15) Notice that it is God mercy and compassion that is being emphasized here. God has every right to exercise His grace upon anyone He chooses.

Paul next raises the example of Pharaoh to demonstrate his point. God raised him up for His own Divine purposes. God put a man in place that would continually harden his heart and in doing so cause God's glory and power to be displayed. And God knew in advance what Pharaoh would do. Pharaoh's stubborn resistance allowed God to make Himself known through the plagues and the opening of the Red Sea so that all the nations might know His glory and power.

There are those who remind us that we are also told that God hardened Pharaoh's heart (Exodus 4:21). How does that work? C. I. Scofield writes, "Instrumentally God hardened Pharaoh's heart by forcing him to an issue against which he hardened his own heart in refusal." 13 As the Greeks used to say, "Whom the gods would destroy, him they make mad."

In the early days of microwave cooking, a friend of mine decided to cook a raw egg still in the shell in his microwave. Of course the egg exploded making a terrible mess. Pharaoh was like that – God turned up the heat and Pharaoh exploded. In that sense one might say, God hardened Pharaoh's heart. But God did not have to decree Pharaoh's response, nor force him to stubborn resistance. Pharaoh bears the full guilt of his actions, but God placed him in the microwave, knowing full well what he would do.

Paul's final illustration is from the potter's wheel. In the illustration of the potter, once again it is God's mercy and long suffering that is emphasized by the writer.

Hath not the potter power over the clay, of the same lump to make one vessel unto honour, and another unto dishonour? What if God, willing to shew his wrath, and to make his power known, endured with much longsuffering the vessels of wrath fitted to destruction: And that he might make known the riches of his glory on the vessels of mercy, which he had afore prepared unto glory, Even us, whom he hath called, not of the Jews only, but also of the Gentiles? (Romans 9:21 – 24)

The idea expressed in verse twenty one is perhaps better understood by looking at the International Standard Version translation; *A potter has the right to do what he wants to with his clay, doesn't he? He can make something for a special occasion or something for ordinary use from the same lump.* Paul used this same simile in 2 Timothy 2:20 where he refers to the contrast between vessels (believers) used exclusively for high and holy things, and those that are fitted for only menial service. Here Paul makes it clear that the way the Lord of the house uses the vessel is up to the vessel, *If a man therefore purge himself from these* (i.e., the sins mentioned in verses 16 – 18), *he shall be a vessel unto honor, sanctified, and meet for the master's use, and prepared unto every good work.*

Here in Romans Paul is emphasizing the grace God has placed on the *vessels of mercy,* both Jew and Gentile, who are called of God, while He continues to exercise His patience upon those *vessels of wrath, fitted to destruction.* In both instances it is the mercy and grace of God that Paul is focusing on.

- **God's Future Mercy to Israel 9:25 – 29**

Paul's final appeal in this section is to the prophet Hosea. He quotes here from two passages, Hosea 2:23; and Hosea 1:10. Both of these passages ring with the assurance of God that Israel will one day be restored and come to faith.

The first passage is sometimes mistakenly applied to the Gentiles, but the context makes it clear that the one formerly rejected (Israel – *not my people*), will one day be again restored. God had "put away" (divorced) His people just as Hosea had his adulterous wife. But just as the prophet pursued his wife, and at the lowest point of her life purchased her back out of her debauchery and ultimately restored her to himself, so God says of Israel, *in the place where it was said unto them, Ye are not my people; there shall they be called the children of the living God.*

The further quotes are all meant to establish the premise of verse six, *For they are not all Israel which are of Israel.* Each of the passages sighted demonstrate that there has always been a "natural Israel" and a "spiritual Israel," – an Israel born after the flesh and an Israel that was born of the Spirit.

Israel's Present: Under Divine Discipline: Romans 9:30 – 10:21

- **Israel's Search for Righteousness 9:30 -- 33**

Paul begins by contrasting the Jewish search for righteousness (right standing with God), with that of the Gentiles. The Gentiles, he tells us, obtained it by faith (just as Abraham did). But the Jews continue to seek righteousness through their observance of the Mosaic Law (and the scores of additional precepts they had added by tradition), and in all their effort, failed to find it. Thus they rejected the righteousness that is available through faith in Christ alone and stumbled at the simplicity of *"he that believeth on him shall not be ashamed* (or disappointed)." (vs.33)

- **The Source and Path to Righteousness 10:1 – 17**

Paul continues this theme as he enters chapter ten, with a reference to his own strong desire and prayer to God for Israel. The sum of the matter is found in verse four; *"For Christ is the end of the Law for righteousness to everyone that believeth."* The Law literally ended in Christ – He fulfilled all its demands and then took all its curse. The Law also ended historically as a Dispensational period of testing. *The grace of God that bringeth salvation hath appeared unto all men. . .* (Titus 2:11). We are now in the Dispensation of Grace.

There follows then a contrast between that righteousness which comes by faith and that righteousness that is offered (but never attainable) by Law. The simplicity of the gospel is set forth; *That if thou shalt confess with thy mouth Jesus as Lord and shalt believe in thine heart that God hath raised Him from the dead, thou shalt be saved . . . for whosoever shall call upon the name of the Lord, shall be saved* (Romans 10:9, 13).

Paul then declares that God makes no difference between the Jew and the Gentile, but is; *rich unto all who call upon Him* (Romans 10:12) Once again it is God's willingness to save that is emphasized.

- **Israel's Failure and Discipline 10:18 – 21**

From verse eighteen through the end of the chapter Paul discusses the fact that Israel has heard. Israel, as well as the rest of mankind, has been confronted by (1) the Word of God (vs.17), and (2) the revelation of nature (vs. 18), but Israel has not obeyed the gospel. So God is using the Gentiles to provoke Israel to jealousy, with a goal of making them desire the blessings that Gentiles are now enjoying. Furthermore, their own prophets foretold that God would do this. But alas, Paul must conclude this section with a quotation from Isaiah 65:2 *All day long I have stretched forth my hands unto a disobedient and gainsaying people.* Again we catch in the agony of those words the heart of God for His disobedient covenant people. God's hand is stretched out, but Israel as a nation has refused.

Israel's Future: God's Purposes & Promises Fulfilled: Romans 11:1 –32

- ## A Believing Remnant – Israel's Blindness is not Total 11:1 – 6

Having ended chapter ten on such a dismal note, the opening question of chapter eleven comes very naturally; *I say then, hath God cast away His people?* – a question that many through the years and even in our day have answered in the affirmative despite Paul's ringing denial; *God forbid*!

Paul will now set forth two premises. First, he will argue that Israel's blindness is not total – there is and has always been a remnant according to the election of grace. Secondly, Paul will declare that Israel's blindness is not final – *all Israel will be saved.* How he draws these two conclusions we will now see.

First Paul begins by demonstrating that there is, and has always been, an elect remnant within Israel who have been faithful to God. Paul reminds his readers that he himself is a Jew and that there were many more at that time who, like himself, had trusted Christ and who believe. Secondly, he reminds them of God's word to Elijah, when the prophet was sure that he stood alone on God's side for righteousness; *I have reserved to myself seven thousand men, who have not bowed the knee to the image of Baal.* The point is that the existence of a faithful remnant proves that God has not "cast away His people."

It is within this passage that we have one of the classic verses on grace found in the Scriptures. Verse six says, *And if by grace, then is it no more of works: otherwise grace is no more grace. But if it be of works, then is it no more grace: otherwise work is no more work.* It is one or the other – grace and works cannot be mixed. Trying to produce the fire of grace by works is like trying to strike a match under water. God's blessings and God's favor are either the result of His gracious choice, or they are a result of something favorable or attractive in us or in something we have done. Paul argues it is never the later, but always the former, and since we are not talking just about His grace toward us as individuals, but His grace toward a nation, it is still and always based upon His elective choice to be gracious. But that nation has rejected His goodness – what now?

- ### Those Who Were Judicially Blinded 11:7 – 10
Israel hath not obtained that which he seeketh for; but the election hath obtained it, and the rest were blinded. (Romans 11:7) Paul argues that there is now a judicial blindness that has fallen over the remainder of the nation and that this too was foreseen by the prophets.

This may be a good time to discuss the matter of blindness as it has to do with men in general. Scripture teaches unequivocally that we are born into this world with a spiritual disorder called blindness. It is impossible for us to see or understand spiritual things. Jesus told Nicodemus, a man well taught in theology and the learning of the day; *Except a man be born again he cannot see the kingdom of God* (John 3:3). Paul wrote, *But the natural man receiveth not the things of the Spirit of God: for they are foolishness unto him: neither can he know them, because they are spiritually discerned.* (1 Corinthians 2:14). This is our condition by natural birth and it might be best described as, "natural blindness" that is blindness to spiritual truth.

But in addition to this, there is a blindness which is imposed by Satan himself upon those who would be given the gospel and seek to know the truth. We read of this in 2 Corinthians 4:3, 4, *But if our gospel be hid, it is hid to them that are lost: In whom the god of this world* (Satan) *hath blinded the minds of them which believe not, lest the light of the glorious gospel of Christ, who is the image of God, should shine unto them.* This may be called *"satanic blindness."* The power of Satan to blind minds is great, but thank God, it is not absolute, and God is able to open spiritual eyes and to shine *in our hearts, to give the light of the knowledge of the glory of God in the face of Jesus Christ* (2 Corinthians 4:6).

However, when there is a stubborn resistance to truth, Scripture describes that as, *"willful blindness."* Addressing the spiritual leaders of Israel Jesus said; *Search the scriptures; for in them ye think ye have eternal life: and they are they which testify of me. And ye will not come to me, that ye might have life* (John 5:39, 40). After all of the evidence of Messiah's death and resurrection, much of the nation of Israel remained adamantly resistant to the gospel and as time went on became so to an increasing degree. It was this condition which resulted in Paul's final closing words to the Jewish community in Rome in the book of Acts (Acts 28:25 – 28).

Israel suffered not only from natural blindness, and satanic blindness, but from that terrible malady called willful blindness, and willful blindness always leads to an act of God called *"judicial blindness."* John predicts this condition in his gospel and quotes a prophecy from Isaiah; *But though he had done so many miracles before them, yet they believed not on him: That the saying of Esaias the prophet might be fulfilled, which he spake, Lord, who hath believed our report? and to whom hath the arm of the Lord been revealed? Therefore they could not believe, because that Esaias said again, He hath blinded their eyes, and hardened their heart; that they should not see with their eyes, nor understand with their heart, and be converted, and I should heal them* (John 12:37 – 40). Willful blindness always leads to judicial blindness and that is what Paul postulates is Israel's present condition.

> *According as it is written, God hath given them the spirit of slumber, eyes that they should not see, and ears that they should not hear;) unto this day. And David saith, Let their table be made a snare, and a trap, and a stumblingblock, and a recompence unto them: Let their eyes be darkened, that they may not see, and bow down their back alway* (Romans 11:8 – 10).

- **Israel's Blindness is not Final 11:11 – 15**

However, at this point Paul's argument takes an interesting turn. He argues that because of Israel's blindness, the light of salvation has come to the Gentiles.

I say then, Have they stumbled that they should fall? God forbid: but rather through their fall salvation is come unto the Gentiles, for to provoke them to jealousy. (Romans 11:11)

Paul now argues that the fall of Israel, that is, their stubborn rejection of the gospel of grace through faith in Christ, has resulted in blessing for the Gentiles. That is a wonderful thing, argues Paul. But if such a blessing could come from their fall, what will happen when they come to their "fullness (πλήρωμα: *pleroma*). This word *pleroma* (fullness) is set in contrast to their "diminishing." It is the same word used in verse twenty five where Paul speaks of the fullness of the Gentiles, i.e., the full number of the Gentiles that will be brought into God's favor during the period of Israel's blindness.

The word, *pleroma* used here, means *what fills up, or completes anything.* Thus, it is applied to what fills a vessel or cup. Barnes writes, "Here it stands opposed to their fall, and their diminution, and evidently means their complete restoration to the favor of God; their recovery from unbelief and apostasy. The apostle then proceeds to show that there will be such a recovery." 14

Paul tells us that he himself is earnestly striving through this situation to use it as an occasion to *provoke to emulation* his Jewish brethren. The new Contemporary English Version (CEV) translates that statement, *make some of my own people jealous enough to be saved.*

Paul speaks of his desire to make Israel hungry for the blessings God is pouring out upon the Gentiles through the gospel. And he further reasons that, *if the casting away of them be the reconciling of the world, what shall the receiving of them be, but life from the dead?* (Romans 11:15) To restate the proposition, when Israel turned their back on God, a door was opened so that the rest of the people in the world were enabled to turn to him. So when Israel returns to God, it will be like bringing the dead back to life.

Two similes are used in this next verse, and because these verses are so very critical to our understanding of this subject we will try to examine each of them very carefully. Each of these two similes is drawn from the Old Testament law of consecrated things;

> *For if the firstfruit be holy, the lump is also holy:*
> *and if the root be holy, so are the branches.*

As regards the reference to the *"Firstfruit"*, Israelites were required to offer to God the first-fruits of the earth - both a sheave of newly ripened grain (Leviticus 23:10, 11), and later, when made into flour, cakes of dough as offerings (Numbers 15:19-21). By these initial offerings of a small portion of the whole, the entire harvest was considered consecrated as was the entire lump of dough from which the offering was made.

So the analogy here – if the patriarchs, Abraham, Isaac, and Jacob (they were the Firstfruits), were set apart for God, then by extension of the Old Testament Law of consecration, the entire offspring is considered consecrated.

- **The Olive Tree and the Branches 11:16 – 25**

The same logic is applied in the analogy of the root and the branches – the consecration of the one extends to the other. Hence Paul is arguing here that all Israel has been particularly consecrated to God. In other words, the Branches that have come out of the root have a right to the blessings of the root.

But is it critical that we define Paul's use of the word "root" here. Is it used as a symbol for the Church as some have supposed? Or is it Abraham that is meant? Or does it go beyond that? In trying to determine the proper usage of a Scriptural symbol, it is important to look for a clear definition in Scripture itself. I am therefore driven to two passages to determine the answer to this question.

In Isaiah chapter eleven, the prophet begins by telling us that a rod shall come out of the stem of Jesse and a Branch shall grow out of his roots (verse 1). The "rod" speaks of sovereignty, hence the prophecy looks forward to the Messiah. But in verse ten we read, *And in that day there shall be a root of Jesse, which shall stand for an ensign of the people; to it shall the Gentiles seek: and his rest shall be glorious.* Here, Messiah is not the "rod" of Jesse, but the "root". In other words, he is before – He Himself is the origin of it all.

Over in the book of Revelation, the title, "the Root of David" is used in chapter five; *And one of the elders said unto me, Weep not: behold, the Lion of the tribe of Judah, the Root of David, hath prevailed to open the book, and to loose the seven seals thereof* (Revelation 5:5). Taking the two verses together, I would conclude that Christ is the "Root" of the Olive Tree and therefore the source of its fatness and blessing (Isaiah 11:10; Rev.5:5).

The "fatness" spoken of in Romans 11:17, must then refer to the blessings which come out of a connection to the root which are, at least in part, a new heart, a new Spirit, and a new relationship to God. But these are precisely the blessings of the New Covenant God promised to Israel so it would appear that the "fatness" or blessings of the New Covenant are what Paul is speaking of here. And those blessings then, flow out of the Root, that is Christ Himself.

But the New Covenant was made with Israel, yet the Gentile branches are enjoying its blessings. How do we Gentiles then come into its blessings? We are but "wild branches" outside any relationship to the Covenants. In another place Paul had written that we Gentiles arc; *aliens from the commonwealth of Israel, and strangers from the covenants of promise* (Ephesians 2:12). But we partake of the blessings of the New Covenant through our relationship to the Mediator of the Covenant, Jesus Christ. Through faith in Him, we are thus "grafted into the Root"(Christ Himself).

Hence we, are partakers of the blessings of the New Covenant, even though it was not made directly with us, for those blessing flow out of Christ Himself. We Gentiles have now been invited to the table of blessing and are invited to partake of Him in these words: *For I have received of the Lord what which also I delivered unto you, That the Lord Jesus the same night in which he was betrayed took bread. . . .After the same manner also he took the cup, when he had supped, saying, This cup is the New Covenant in my blood: this do ye, as oft as ye drink it, in remembrance of me* (1 Corinthians 11:23- 25). What a privileged place we have been given and we should now be bringing forth the fruit of the blessed position we enjoy.

But while the New Covenant has been established in the blood of the Covenant Maker Himself, and thus is blessings are available to those who are connected to Him, what of the branches that will not live and draw upon the root? What if they become, dried up and dead? That is exactly what happened to Israel.

It was early in Paul's ministry that he encountered this resistance on the part of the Jews. As soon as he was converted his life was threatened by the Jews so that he had to escape from Damascus in a basket let down from a window. In Antioch of Pisidia Paul met Jewish opposition with the words, *It was necessary that the word of God should first have been spoken to you* (Jews): *but seeing ye put it from you, and judge yourselves unworthy of everlasting life, lo, we turn to the Gentiles* (Acts 13:46).

It was the Jews who stirred up the opposition against the gospel message in Thessalonica (Acts 17:5 – 9). In Corinth it was the same; *And when Silas and Timotheus were come from Macedonia, Paul was pressed in the spirit, and testified to the Jews that Jesus was Christ. And when they opposed themselves, and blasphemed, he shook his raiment, and said unto them, Your blood be upon your own heads; I am clean: from henceforth I will go unto the Gentiles.* (Acts 18:5, 6).

In Ephesus Paul, *went into the synagogue* (of the Jews), *and spake boldly for the space of three months, disputing and persuading the things concerning the kingdom of God. But when divers were hardened, and believed not, but spake evil of that way before the multitude, he departed from them, and separated the disciples, disputing daily in the school of one Tyrannus*—a Gentile. (Acts 19:8, 9).

It was against the accusations of the Jews that Paul had to defend both himself and his gospel to Gentile kings and finally to Caesar himself, and it is not without significance that the closing words of the book of Acts read;

> *And when they* (the Jews) *had appointed him a day, there came many to him into his lodging; to whom he expounded and testified the kingdom of God, persuading them concerning Jesus, both out of the law of Moses, and out of the prophets, from morning till evening. And some believed the things which were spoken, and some believed not. And when they agreed not among themselves, they departed, after that Paul had spoken one word; Well spake the Holy Ghost by Esaias the prophet unto our fathers, Saying, Go unto this people, and say, Hearing ye shall hear, and shall not understand; and seeing ye shall see, and not perceive: For the heart of this people is waxed gross, and their ears are dull of hearing, and their eyes have they closed; lest they should see with their eyes, and hear with their ears, and understand with their heart, and should be converted, and I should heal them. Be it known therefore unto you, that the salvation of God is sent unto the Gentiles, and that they will hear it. And when he had said these words, the Jews departed, and had great reasoning among themselves.* (Acts 28:23 – 29)

Tragically it is often the same today. While there has been a significant movement among the Jewish people in our time and there are many Messianic Jews who confess Jesus (Yeshua) as their Lord and Savior, and an increasing number who are bearing testimony to Him, it is nevertheless painfully true that the vast majority among the natural seed of Abraham are completely blind to the gospel and resistant to its appeal.

In the new State of Israel, orthodox and conservative forces have framed laws to keep the gospel message from freely going forth, and individual Jews often persecute those who would spread the gospel message. Israel dwells today in a state of alienation from God and His gospel and Paul answers by saying, *some of the branches are broken off.* This is not a new idea. Paul is again drawing on a well known Old Testament simile. Both Jeremiah and Isaiah had spoken of the same.

Jeremiah wrote, *The LORD called thy name, A green olive tree, fair, and of goodly fruit: with the noise of a great tumult he hath kindled fire upon it, and the branches of it are broken.* (Jeremiah 11:16)

And Isaiah says, *When the boughs thereof are withered, they shall be broken off: the women come, and set them on fire: for it is a people of no understanding: therefore he that made them will not have mercy on them, and he that formed them will shew them no favour.* (Isaiah 27:11)

And our Lord himself declared to Israel, *The kingdom of God shall be taken from you, and given to a nation* (ethnos: people), *bringing forth the fruits thereof.* (Matthew 21:43) Like the fig tree upon which our Lord found no fruit, Israel had become a fruitless branch and was therefore broken off from the Olive tree of blessing.

But there is a bright side to this tragedy. The Jewish nation cut themselves out of the tree of blessing and their fall from God's favor has been tragic, but it also has a bright side. Through Israel's refusal, God is now freely offering to the Gentiles His favor and hence we read; *And if some of the branches be broken off, and thou, being a wild olive tree, wert grafted in among them, and with them partakest of the root and fatness of the olive tree* (Romans 11:17). Yes, through Israel's "breaking off", we Gentiles have been grafted in and partake of the blessings of the root (Christ).

That is precisely Paul's point in Ephesians when he writes; *Wherefore remember, that ye being in time past Gentiles in the flesh, who are called Uncircumcision by that which is called the Circumcision in the flesh made by hands; That at that time ye were without Christ, being aliens from the commonwealth of Israel, and strangers from the covenants of promise, having no hope, and without God in the world: But now in Christ Jesus ye who sometimes were far off are made nigh by the blood of Christ* (Ephesians 2:11 – 13).

Strangers from the covenants, aliens from Israel, having no hope – what a description of our former condition. But now, we have been grafted into the place of blessing and are part with the "Root" itself for *they which are of faith, the same are the children of Abraham.* What a blessing! What a place of privilege has been accorded us.

It is necessary to note here that the Gentiles are referred to as being cut off from, *the olive tree which is wild by nature* (verse 24). This kind of grafting is not usual. It is usual for a good scion to be grafted into a wild tree and the wild tree then gives nourishment to a good branch. But it is never done in reverse as Paul here acknowledges, *For if thou wert cut out of the olive tree which is wild by nature, and wert graphed <u>contrary to nature</u> into a good olive tree* (verse 24).

Vincent, in his word studies cites Dr. Thomson ("Land and Book, Lebanon, Damascus and Beyond Jordan," p. 35) as follows: "In the kingdom of nature generally, certainly in the case of the olive, the process referred to by the apostle never succeeds. Graft the good upon the wild, and, as the Arabs say, 'it will conquer the wild;' but you cannot reverse the process with success.... It is only in the kingdom of grace that a process thus contrary to nature can be successful; and it is this circumstance which the apostle has seized upon to magnify the mercy shown to the Gentiles by grafting them, a wild race, contrary to the nature of such operations, into the good olive tree . . ., and causing them to flourish there and bring forth fruit unto eternal life. The apostle lived in the land of the olive, and was in no danger of falling into a blunder in founding his argument upon such a circumstance in its cultivation." 15

Having seen then that the process used by the Apostle to illustrate what has occurred is a process of pure grace, Paul then warns against the very tendency which is so consistently displayed by a large portion of Christendom to this day, that is, the tendency to assume that we are now the privileged ones and that God has no further use for Israel. Paul warns us against just such a conclusion: *Boast not against the branches. But if thou boast, thou bearest not the root, but the root thee. Thou wilt say then, The branches were broken off, that I might be grafted in. Well; because of unbelief they were broken off, and thou standest by faith. Be not highminded, but fear: For if God spared not the natural branches,* (Israel) *take heed lest he also spare not thee* (Gentiles). *Behold therefore the goodness and severity of God: on them which fell, severity; but toward thee, goodness, if thou continue in his goodness: otherwise thou also shalt be cut off* (Romans 11:17 – 22).

- **Israel will be Grafted In Again 11:23 -- 25**

The reason for Israel's rejection and "cutting off" was her unbelief and fruitlessness. The divine husbandman looks for branches that bear fruit. But the New Testament predicts, and we are seeing it happen all around us, that there will be a time when the same hardness and blindness and unbelief that characterized Israel, will come upon the Gentiles (1 Timothy 4:1, 2; 2 Timothy 3:1 – 8; 4:3, 4; 2 Peter 2; 1 John 2:18, 19; Jude; Revelation 3:14 – 19).

When that happens God will surely take away our part out of the tree of blessing and, according to Paul, *if thou wert cut out of the olive tree which is wild by nature, and wert grafted contrary to nature into a good olive tree: how much more shall these, which be the natural branches, be grafted into their own olive tree?* (Romans 11:14). It is impossible to miss the point here. The whole argument of these verses began with the question; Hath God cast away His people (Israel)? That is, is God done with them forever, and the Holy Spirit through the Apostle gives a resounding "no" to that question.

The Apostle sums it up in verse twenty five; *For I would not, brethren, that ye should be ignorant of this mystery, lest ye should be wise in your own conceits; that blindness in part is happened to Israel, until the fullness of the Gentiles be come in.* There are two things we need to notice in this verse. First, the blindness of Israel is not total. There is at this very time a remnant according to the election of grace. The second thing we must notice is that this temporary blindness is not final. It will last until *the fullness of the Gentiles be come in*, that is until the full number of those from among the Gentiles have been gathered.

That is what is happening during this Dispensation of Grace. That is what was noted in Acts 15 as God's program; *God at the first* (i.e., for the first time) *did visit the Gentiles to take out of them a people for his name* (Acts 15:14). That harvest is what has characterized this age (Matthew 13). But that harvest will someday end, and then the promise will be fulfilled; *And if I go and prepare a place for you I will come again and receive you unto myself, that where I am there ye may be also* (John 14:3; compare 1 Thessalonians 4:13 – 18). The Church will be Raptured and God will again turn His attention on Israel.

- **All Israel will be Saved 11:26 – 32**

Now Paul declares the matter unequivocally, *And so all Israel shall be saved: as it is written, There shall come out of Zion the Deliverer, and shall turn away ungodliness from Jacob.* This is not a fond wish on the part of the Apostle, but a firm promise written in both the Old Testament and the New Testament. And Israel still means Israel, some of our Replacement Theology friends to the contrary notwithstanding.

It is not altogether possible to define strictly how the "all Israel" should be interpreted. Paul makes a distinction between spiritual Israel and natural Israel in this same passage. It may be that we can understand it better as we look at relevant OT prophecies such as the one in Zechariah eleven where the Holy Spirit reveals that in the future time of Israel's trouble, sometimes referred to as the Great Tribulation: *it shall come to pass, that in all the land, saith the LORD, two parts therein shall be cut off and die; but the third shall be left therein. And I will bring the third part through the fire, and will refine them as silver is refined, and will try them as gold is tried: they shall call on my name, and I will hear them: I will say, It is my people: and they shall say, The LORD is my God* (Zechariah 11:8, 9).

Here, according to Zechariah, "all Israel" will amount to about a third of the then existing nation. Whatever it means in precise terms however, the certainty of the final conversion of Israel as a people is guaranteed.

Paul then moves immediately to what under girds that promise, that is, the covenant and specifically what we have referred to as the New Covenant. *For this is my covenant unto them, when I shall take away their sins.* (Romans 11:27). That is the promise of the New Covenant, and it is that promise Paul assures us will be fulfilled. Please notice it is not "if" I shall take away, but "when". The covenant is as sure today as it was the day it was made.

We have already seen that the Covenant was initiated and ratified in the blood of the Messiah, as it must be, for it promises the transformation that faith in Yeshua brings. We, both Jews and Gentiles, who have placed our faith in Him, are brought into the blessings of that covenant and we celebrate it each time we gather around the Lord's table to remember Him.

But the covenant's exact terms can only be fulfilled with the House of Israel and its ultimate fulfillment awaits the time when Israel as a people will be brought in under the benefits and blessing of the covenant. It is that which the Apostle refers to then in verses twenty eight and twenty nine. *As concerning the gospel, they are enemies for your sakes: but as touching the election,* (God's sovereign determinate choice), *they are beloved for the fathers' sakes. For the gifts and calling of God are without repentance.*

Theologian Ronald Diprose concluded his careful study of the Romans passage like this:

In the light of the conclusion in v. 28, we can safely say that Paul also is confirming the election of Israel despite the nation's failure to recognize Jesus as their Messiah. Nothing, not even their opposition to the gospel, could cancel the special love of God for his people. <u>It is this election of Israel which makes her eschatological salvation certain.</u> 16

I love that final statement, *For the gifts and calling of God are without repentance.* In our vernacular, God doesn't change His mind about His elective choices, or as we said earlier, God never says, Whoops! Did He choose Israel and set His love upon them. Then He will most certainly fulfill to them all of His good purposes, their stubbornness and unbelief, notwithstanding. As we observed earlier, God's purposes are never frustrated by man's failures, nor are they at the mercy of man's performance.

Paul concludes his argument with these words; *For as ye in times past have not believed God, yet have now obtained mercy through their unbelief: Even so have these also now not believed, that through your mercy they also may obtain mercy. For God hath concluded them all in unbelief, that he might have mercy upon all.*

Jonathan Edwards wrote of this passage;

> Nothing is more certainly foretold than this national conversion of the Jews is in the eleventh chapter of Romans. And there are also many passages of the Old Testament that can't be interpreted in any other sense. Besides the prophecies of the calling of the Jews, we have a remarkable seal of the fulfillment of this great event in providence by a kind of continual miracle, viz. the preserving them a distinct [nation] when in such a dispersed condition for above sixteen hundred years. The world affords nothing else like it – a remarkable hand of providence. 17

Then having drawn his conclusion, the Apostle launches into a spontaneous doxology of praise that is one of the most moving in all the Word of God:

> *O the depth of the riches both of the wisdom and knowledge of God! how unsearchable are his judgments, and his ways past finding out! For who hath known the mind of the Lord? or who hath been his counselor? Or who hath first given to him, and it shall be recompensed unto him again? For of him, and through him, and to him, are all things: to whom be glory for ever. Amen.*

What can possibly be added? We have sought to discover whether the Scriptures predict with absolute certainty a future spiritual conversion for the Nation Israel, and we have seen in the Covenants - in the Prophets - and in the New Testament Epistle, there is a non ambiguous concert of certainty regarding that event. But what could possibly happen that could bring it to pass. What would it take to transform Israel's stubborn unbelief into a humble repentant faith in her Messiah Savior? Perhaps a look at the conversion of the first Israel might help.

SECTION TWO:

THE CIRCUMSTANCES

OF ISRAEL'S CONVERSION

CHAPTER FIVE : The Conversion of the first Israel

Perhaps this seems at first glance like a strange subject to be discussing within the context of the conversion of a nation. What, you might ask, has the experience of Jacob to do with the future experience of the nation which derives its name from him? Possibly more than we would think.

There are a number of historic events in the history of Abraham's descendants which prefigure events that will occur in Israel's future. Few would deny that the historical record of Joseph creates a tapestry that pre-figures the Messiah. Dr. C. I. Scofield writes:

> "While it is nowhere asserted that Joseph was a type of Christ, the analogies are too numerous to be accidental. They are: (1) both were especial objects of a father's love (Genesis 37:3); (Matthew 3:17); (John 3:35); (John 5:20). (2) both were hated by their brethren (Genesis 37:4); (John 15:25). (3) the superior claims of both were rejected by their brethren (Genesis 37:8); (Matthew 21:37-39); (John 15:24); (John 15:25). (4) the brethren of both conspired against them to slay them (Gen_37:18); (Mat_26:3); (Matthew 26:4). (5) Joseph was, in intent and figure, slain by his brethren, as was Christ (Genesis 37:24); (Matthew 27:35-37). (6) each became a blessing among the Gentiles, and gained a Gentile bride (Genesis 41:1-45); (Acts 15:14); (Ephesians 5:25-32). (7) as Joseph reconciled his brethren to himself, and afterward

exalted them, so will it be with Christ and His Jewish brethren (Genesis 45:1-15); (Deuteronomy 30:1-10); (Hosea 2:14-18); (Romans 11:1, 15, 25, 26)." 18

Other grand events of the Patriarchs lives prefigure greater events in the future. We all recognize Abraham's sacrifice of Isaac on Mount Moriah as a prefigure of the sacrifice of God's own Son on the same mount many years later. The great event prefigured an even greater, which is true in each case. It is a seminal event in the life of a Patriarch and becomes a prefigure of a much greater event in the later experience of the nation.

Scofield has a further note on Jacob's years in Haran. He writes,

> "Jacob at Haran becomes a sterling illustration, if not type, of the nation descended from him in its present long dispersion. Like Israel, he was: (1) Out of the place of blessing (Genesis 26:3). (2) without an altar (Hosea 3:4, 5). (3) gained an evil name (Genesis 31:1); (Romans 2:17-24). (4) but was under the covenant care of Jehovah (Genesis 28:13, 14); (Romans 11:1, 25-30). (5) and was ultimately brought back (Genesis 31:3); (Genesis 35:1-4); (Ezekiel 37:21-23). The personal lesson is obvious: while Jacob is not forsaken, he is permitted to reap the shame and sorrow of his self-chosen way." 19

These several illustrations should help us get hold of this principle, that God sometimes prefigures the path of the nation in the experience of its patriarchs. Hence then, the importance of studying the conversion of the original Israel.

A study of the life of Jacob is most instructive and illuminating. It can be argued that Jacob possessed, early in his life, some sense of the Eternal and placed a value upon the covenant blessings to which, as the elder son, his brother Esau would most naturally have been heir. Or is that reading too much into it? Is Jacob only seeing the birthright as a prize for advancing his own ambitions? I do not believe it is possible to really know what his motivations were, but his actions, though dubious, were moving him in a drama whose ending was determined by God: *"For the children being not yet born, neither having done any good or evil, that the purposes of God according to election might stand, not of works, but of him that calleth: It was said unto her, The elder shall serve the younger.* (Romans 9:11, 12)

Jacob's name described his character – he was a self-serving opportunist that put his own interests ahead of everyone and everything else. Having bargained the birthright from Esau for a mere bowl of pottage (lentils), he had then followed his mother's instruction and represented himself to his nearly blind father as being his brother Esau. He thus obtained through subterfuge and deception, the blessing of the Patriarch, which carried with it the Covenant blessings of his grandfather Abraham.

Our sensibilities are rightly appalled by such blatant rascality. We wonder why God would (or could), ever do anything with Jacob, but watch His methods, watch His ways. V. Raymond Edman meditates on that in *The Disciplines of Life,* page 54:

> When God wants to drill a man,
> And thrill a man, And skill a man,
> When God wants to mold a man
> To play the noblest part;
> When He yearns with all His heart
> To create so great and bold a man
> That all the world shall be amazed,
> Watch His methods, watch His ways!
>
> How He ruthlessly perfects
> Whom He royally elects!
> How He hammers him and hurts him,
> And with mighty blows converts him
> Into trial shapes of clay which
> Only God understands;
> While his tortured heart is crying
> And he lifts beseeching hands!

How He bends but never breaks
When his good He undertakes;
How He uses whom He chooses,
And with every purpose fuses him;
By every act induces him
To try His splendor out -
God knows what He's about. 20

Esau was enraged and determined to thwart the entire scheme by killing his brother as soon as his father died. Caught in the web of his own scheming duplicity Jacob fled the hostility of his brother who was looking for an opportunity to slay him.

On the way to his self-imposed exile, he met for the first time the God of whom his father Isaac had spoken (Genesis 28). It was an amazing and impressive encounter, and deeply impressed Jacob so that he made a kind of commitment to God that if He would watch over him and prosper him, he would acknowledge and own Him as his very own God. There is debate among expositors about the depth of Jacob's commitment at this point. Some believe that this is the point of his spiritual conversion. As the English are wont to say, "the proof is in the pudding." There is little evidence that anything in Jacob's character changed as a result of his encounter at Bethel.

In exile Jacob faced the very kind of duplicity in his master Laban that he himself had demonstrated in his dealings with Esau and with Isaac. First his intended bride is exchanged on the night of his wedding and he wakes to find himself with the older sister, Leah. Then he is forced to labor seven additional years for his beloved Rachel. As he watches the flocks and herds of Laban, he attempts to gain his own livestock through six more years of labor. Each time he makes progress, his wages are changed.

For twenty years Jacob labored under the most adverse conditions. He would sum it all up to Laban at the last in these words: *These twenty years have I been with thee . . . the rams of thy flock have I not eaten. That which was torn of beasts I brought not unto thee; I bare the loss of it; of my hand didst thou require it, whether stolen by day, or stolen by night. Thus I was; in the day the drought consumed me, and the frost by night; and my sleep departed from mine eyes . . . Except the God of my father, the God of Abraham, and the fear of Isaac, had been with me, surely thou hadst sent me away now empty.* (Genesis 31:38 – 42)

It was not personal preference that drew Jacob back to the Land, however, but the mandate of God (Genesis 31:3). The God of Bethel had been with him, though Jacob had continued to scheme and try to manipulate things to his own advantage. Jacob's consciousness of God increased, but his commitment to God is still in question.

It seems evident to me that while Jacob's recognition of God's providential care and involvement in his life grew as time went on, Jacob never really turned his whole heart to God until, upon his return from Mesopotamia, he wrestled alone with God at Peniel. It was here in the desperation of the greatest threat he had ever faced that Jacob, at long last, knew his own helplessness, his deplorable condition and his need of God. It was here God changed both his name and his character.

Jacob had sent his servants to greet Esau and to discern the safety of returning to the Land which he had so long ago forsaken. The servants had returned with an alarming report; *We came to thy brother Esau, and also he cometh to meet thee, and four hundred men with him. Then Jacob was greatly afraid and distressed* (Genesis 32:6, 7). Jacob knew what his brother was capable of and now his worst fears were confirmed. Meeting Esau would mean a massacre, and he could not risk a battle with Esau. His covenant with Laban at Mizpah made a return to Haran impossible – there was no one but God to turn to.

In preparation for his encounter at Peniel, Jacob prayed and interestingly he pled the covenant made with Abraham and affirmed to his father Isaac;

And Jacob said, O God of my father Abraham, and God of my father Isaac, the LORD which saidst unto me, Return unto thy country, and to thy kindred, and I will deal well with thee: I am not worthy of the least of all the mercies, and of all the truth, which thou hast shewed unto thy servant; for with my staff I passed over this Jordan; and now I am become two bands. Deliver me, I pray thee, from the hand of my brother, from the hand of Esau: for I fear him, lest he will come and smite me, and the mother with the children. And thou saidst, I will surely do thee good, and make thy seed as the sand of the sea, which cannot be numbered for multitude (Genesis 32:9 – 12).

That Jacob has recognized God and His dealings with him is evident. I believe this prayer shows Jacob's first grasp of God's grace, his first realization of his own unworthiness. He must now be made to face himself – he must see himself for who and what he is.

There at Peniel Jacob wrestled alone with God – quite literally. Subsequent Scripture makes clear that the One he wrestled with was none other than the Angel of the LORD, the pre-incarnate Christ. As if his situation where not bad enough, the One he wrestled with and resisted further weakened him by touching the hollow of his thigh. Until now, in the face of any such imminent threat, if he could not have fought, at least he might have run. Now even that possibility is taken from him. In the face of such impending danger he could only hobble, like the poor cripple he had now become.

So in the face of his condition he was driven by the circumstances of his case and of the impossible danger that lay before him to cry out for the mercy and grace of God – *I will not let Thee go except Thou bless me* he cried. His wrestling was over, but in his desperation faith took over and he cried out for God in the darkest hour of his sordid career. He could no longer wrestle – he could only hold on in a death grip of desperation.

Now, at long last, he was forced by the Angel's question to acknowledge painfully who and what he was: *My name is Jacob . . . heel catcher, cheat, grasper . . .* all the ugly, ugly truth of a character completely other than what God would have him to be. He was self serving, a deceiver, a schemer in every way, and now he must come at last to face himself in all his shame and Jacob abhorred what he saw. How painful was it for Jacob to speak those words . . . "My name is Jacob?" It was not only a response, it was a confession, and God responded, as He always does, when we come to the end of ourselves.

God's own commentary on this event is recorded by Hosea; *He took his brother by the heel in the womb, and by his strength he had power with God: Yea, he had power over the angel, and prevailed: he wept, and made supplication unto him: he found him in Bethel, and there he spake with us; Even the LORD God of hosts; the LORD is his memorial.* (Hosea 12:2 – 5). In the moment he surrendered he prevailed. At the point he stopped struggling and simply held onto God he was transformed.

Some have questioned that this experience really marks Jacob's conversion. Some point to previous experiences Jacob had with God to tell us that what happened here was not that different – but I would disagree.

When a Simon becomes a Peter we say he was converted. When a Saul becomes a Paul, we say the same. When a Jacob, with all the meaning his name possessed, becomes Israel, a prince with God, and when it is God Himself (who knows his heart), that changes his name, I would argue, that is the moment of his conversion.

So what drove the self reliant Jacob to his face in repentance and faith? What changed him from the schemer Jacob to Israel, "a Prince with God?" Obviously, it was the Sovereignty and intervention of God. From a more human standpoint however, it was the threat of an angry brother with an army coming against him. Jacob recognized Esau's army was so superior that he was helpless against it. Helplessness is a wonderful preparation for spiritual blessing.

And what do the prophets tell us will bring the Nation Israel, that stubborn, stiff-necked, arrogant, self sufficient nation to repentance and faith? Is it not possible that there will be a reenactment of Jacob's conversion that will cause Israel to acknowledge who and what she has been and cry out for mercy from the only One who could possibly keep her from utter annihilation? I believe it will be exactly that! Just as the conversion of Saul *as one born out of the due time* (*ektromah;* 1 Corinthians 15:8), became a pre-picture of the ultimate conversion of the nation, so the experience of Israel, the very Patriarch whose name that nation bears, is a miniature of that conversion which is to come under similar (though vastly greater) circumstances.

Stanley Ellison expresses it well,

> "Israel's basic need today is not peace with the Arabs, it is peace with God. . . A historic tryst with her covenant Lord similar to that of Jacob returning from exile" 21

I believe prophecy indicates that is exactly what Israel will have. And it will come about at a time when, just like Jacob, Israel will be helpless before the threat of imminent and total destruction.

CHAPTER SIX: Examining the Circumstances of Israel's Future Conversion

The Scriptures predict, in a number of places, a great invasion of the land of Israel in the latter days. Actually there are two invasions and they need to be distinguished if we are to understand the events of this period. The invasion we are speaking of is not Armageddon, though it is often mistaken for that conflict. The invasion here is an earlier one and involves very specific nations and peoples. The key passage for this study is Ezekiel 36:16-39:29.

I am persuaded that the central theme of this entire section is often missed or misunderstood. The central theme is not the battle, as important as that is to the story. The central theme is the spiritual rebirth of Israel (see Ezekiel 36:24-27; 37:9, 14; 39:22, 28-29). Chapter thirty six will **declare** it, chapter thirty seven will **describe** it, and chapter thirty eight and thirty nine will **define** the details of how it takes place.

Chapter 36 **declares** what God intends to do and why. God first addresses the "mountains of Israel." They are desolate and controlled by the nations round about. Jehovah declares that they will be re-inhabited by Israel once again.

The central message really begins however in verse sixteen:

> *Moreover the word of the LORD came unto me, saying, Son of man, when the house of Israel dwelt in their own land, they defiled it by their own way and by their doings: their way was before me as the uncleanness of a removed woman. Wherefore I*

poured my fury upon them for the blood that they had shed upon the land, and for their idols wherewith they had polluted it: And I scattered them among the heathen, and they were dispersed through the countries: according to their way and according to their doings I judged them. And when they entered unto the heathen, whither they went, they profaned my holy name, when they said to them, These are the people of the LORD, and are gone forth out of his land. But I had pity for mine holy name, which the house of Israel had profaned among the heathen, whither they went (Ezekiel 36:16 – 21).

Two things are readily observable. First, God lays out before His people the reasons they have been driven into captivity and dispersed from the Land. This people disgraced (profaned) Jehovah's name while they were in the Land. They have been murderers and idolaters. Secondly, when they were dispersed among the nations, their conduct continued to bring disgrace to that Holy Name with which they were associated.

Jehovah thus makes clear in the next verses that what He is about to do is not because of any merit or desert on the part of Israel, but rather, because His name is associated with this people He will do what He does to vindicate His own Holy Name. He further indicates that when He has done it, all the heathen will know His majesty and His power. Look at verses twenty two and twenty three.

Therefore say unto the house of Israel, Thus saith the Lord GOD; I do not this for your sakes, O house of Israel, but for mine holy name's sake, which ye have profaned among the heathen, whither ye went. And I will sanctify my great name, which was profaned among the heathen, which ye have profaned in the midst of them; and the heathen shall know that I am the LORD, saith

the Lord GOD, when I shall be sanctified in you
before their eyes (Ezekiel 36:22, 23).

It is of greatest importance that we understand this, because the most common objection that is raised against a future for the nation Israel is their utter unworthiness of such a blessing. Interestingly, God agrees. As always, His benefits and blessings will be because of His Grace, and for His own benefit and glory, that is, to protect His own reputation and name.

Beginning in verse twenty four, God outlines what He intends to do and to accomplish in Israel. Look carefully at each of the words:

> *For I will take you from among the heathen, and*
> *gather you out of all countries, and will bring you*
> *into your own land. Then will I sprinkle clean*
> *water upon you, and ye shall be clean: from all*
> *your filthiness, and from all your idols, will I*
> *cleanse you. A new heart also will I give you, and*
> *a new spirit will I put within you: and I will take*
> *away the stony heart out of your flesh, and I will*
> *give you an heart of flesh. And I will put my spirit*
> *within you, and cause you to walk in my statutes,*
> *and ye shall keep my judgments, and do them. And*
> *ye shall dwell in the land that I gave to your*
> *fathers; and ye shall be my people, and I will be*
> *your God* (Ezekiel 36:24 – 28).

Please notice that this prediction reaches beyond any mere Babylonian captivity. Jehovah will gather them out of *all countries*. As we continue in this passage it will become more and more evident that this looks forward to a time yet future in Israel's life. That theme is repeated again before the chapter closes:

> *Not for your sakes do I this, saith the Lord GOD,*
> *be it known unto you: be ashamed and confounded*
> *for your own ways, O house of Israel* (Ezekiel
> 36:32).

Now, chapter thirty seven **describes** in symbolic terms what God will do, and, as noted before, chapters thirty eight and thirty nine will **define** the events which will transpire to bring it to pass.

> *The hand of the LORD was upon me, and carried me out in the spirit of the LORD, and set me down in the midst of the valley which was full of bones, And caused me to pass by them round about: and, behold, there were very many in the open valley; and, lo, they were very dry. And he said unto me, Son of man, can these bones live? And I answered, O Lord GOD, thou knowest. Again he said unto me, Prophesy upon these bones, and say unto them, O ye dry bones, hear the word of the LORD. Thus saith the Lord GOD unto these bones; Behold, I will cause breath to enter into you, and ye shall live: And I will lay sinews upon you, and will bring up flesh upon you, and cover you with skin, and put breath in you, and ye shall live; and ye shall know that I am the LORD.* (Ezekiel 37:1 – 6)

The vision of the prophet is strange indeed and has been the subject of sermons and songs for centuries. However, the basic facts are these; Ezekiel is placed in the midst of a valley that is full of dry bones. The dryness indicates both the fact that they have been a long time in this state and the absolute hopelessness of bringing anything out of this graveyard.

The second thing to note is that Ezekiel is commanded to prophecy (or preach) unto these bones – a task that must have seemed futile indeed. Of course, by way of application it might be noted that any time the Word of God is proclaimed to unsaved individuals, the case is very similar to the picture here. Apart from the breath of redeeming grace blowing upon them through the life-giving Spirit of God, nothing can be accomplished. However, the point here is more specific than that.

Verse eleven clearly identifies the symbolism of the bones; *Son of man, these bones are the whole house of Israel.* (Ezekiel 37:11) What a picture of that nation. Yet up until 1948 it was a perfect picture of Israel. She was cut off from her parts, scattered to every nation under heaven and had been in that case for nearly two thousand years. Then something miraculous happened:

> *So I prophesied as I was commanded: and as I prophesied, there was a noise, and behold a shaking, and the bones came together, bone to his bone. And when I beheld, lo, the sinews and the flesh came up upon them, and the skin covered them above: but there was no breath in them* (Ezekiel 37:7, 8).

National restoration of the nation came about beginning with the rebirth of Israel in 1948. Since that time her "parts" have continued to come together from almost every nation under heaven. Tens of thousands from the four corners of the compass continue to come to the ancient Land allotted them by God. However, there is still a terrible fact – there is no breath in them – that is, they have no real spiritual life.

They are still living in unbelief and rejection of their Messiah and Savior, Jesus Christ. That is their need. As Stanley Ellison said, "Israel's basic need today is not peace with the Arabs, it is peace with God. . . A historic tryst with her covenant Lord similar to that of Jacob returning from exile" (cited chapter 5). Israel needs a new birth and that is exactly what Ezekiel predicts and describes next.

> *Then said he unto me, Prophesy unto the wind, prophesy, son of man, and say to the wind, Thus saith the Lord GOD; Come from the four winds, O breath, and breathe upon these slain, that they may live. So I prophesied as he commanded me, and the breath came into them, and they lived, and stood up upon their feet, an exceeding great army* (Ezekiel 37:9, 10).

Two things are worth noting here: First, Israel will experience a spiritual rebirth brought about by a miraculous act of the Spirit of God. Secondly, once they experience that rebirth, they will not be passive, but will become, *an exceeding great army.* One might ask, "What kind of army will they be?" I think further study will demonstrate that they will be a "Salvation Army" like none ever before them – but that is ahead of our text.

Misunderstanding or misinterpreting this passage is inexcusable because God Himself has explained its meaning in the clearest and most straightforward language.

> *Then he said unto me, Son of man, these bones are the whole house of Israel: behold, they say, Our bones are dried, and our hope is lost: we are cut off for our parts. Therefore prophesy and say unto them, Thus saith the Lord GOD; Behold, O my people, I will open your graves, and cause you to come up out of your graves, and bring you into the land of Israel. And ye shall know that I am the LORD, when I have opened your graves, O my people, and brought you up out of your graves, And shall put my spirit in you, and ye shall live, and I shall place you in your own land: then shall ye know that I the LORD have spoken it, and performed it, saith the LORD* (Ezekiel 37:11 – 14).

Language could hardly be clearer, and please **note:** the events promised and prophesied in this passage have never been experienced by Israel in the past. Never has she experienced the spiritual resurrection that is envisioned in this passage. For those of us who believe that God does not lie and is not limited by anything man does, or does not do, that can only mean one thing – we are talking about a future time – but perhaps not as far in the future as we might think.

This passage should be read carefully, noting that the following symbols are interpreted by the passage itself:

- The bones – the whole house of Israel.
- The graves – the nations where they (Israel) are scattered (dispersed).
- The bones coming together – Israel's return to the Land (Ezekiel 37:12,21).
- No breath in them – they become a national entity, but remain spiritually dead.
- The wind – the Holy Spirit who will bring spiritual regeneration to Israel (Romans 11).

So Ezekiel 36 declares a restoration and conversion, Ezekiel 37 describes that restoration and conversion symbolically (but interpreted literally by the text itself), and Ezekiel 38, 39 defines exactly what will bring Israel's conversion to pass.

The remainder of chapter thirty seven promises the restoration of all of Israel. The miracle of the two sticks, representing Ephraim(the ten northern tribes), and Judah(the two southern tribes), becoming one stick in the prophet's hand was a vivid unmistakable sign that ancient Israel will be once again gathered and united. This promise is referenced in several places in the Old Testament, but none as powerful as the New Testament declaration of the sealing of the 144,000 in the seventh chapter of the book of Revelation. All twelve tribes are to be reunited and the Kingdom glory is seen in some of the closing words of chapter thirty seven. There are seven great promises made to Israel in Chapter thirty seven.

- *I will save them . . . and will cleanse them*: (vs. 23)
- *David my servant shall be king over them* (vs. 24)
- *They shall dwell in the land that I have given unto Jacob my servant wherein your fathers have dwelt* (vs. 25)
- *I will make an everlasting covenant of peace with them;* (vs. 26)
- *I will place them, and multiply them,* (vs. 26)

- *I will set my sanctuary in the midst of them for evermore.* (vs. 28)
- *I will be their God, and they shall be my people.* (vs. 27)

The amazing thing to me is that most expositors separate the promises and predictions of chapters thirty six and thirty seven from the events of chapter thirty eight and thirty nine. But the subject does not change. When we come to the concluding verses of chapter thirty nine we find God talking about the same things He was referencing in chapter thirty six and thirty seven. Here is a list of those closing promises:

- *I will set my glory among the heathen, and all the heathen shall see my judgment that I have executed, and my hand that I have laid upon them.* (vs. 21)
- *The house of Israel shall know that I am the LORD their God from that day and forward.* (vs. 22)
- *The heathen shall know that the house of Israel went into captivity for their iniquity: because they trespassed against me* (verse 23)
- *I will be jealous for my holy name;* (vs. 25) *when I have brought them again from the people, and gathered them out of their enemies' lands, and am sanctified in them in the sight of many nations;* (vs. 27)
- *Neither will I hide my face any more from them: for I have poured out my spirit upon the house of Israel, saith the Lord GOD.*(vs. 29)

What was Jehovah God concerned about in chapter thirty six? It was the defamation of His name that had taken place because of Israel's conduct and because of the judgments He has poured upon them. The heathen nations around Israel could see little difference between Israel's conduct and their own. Further, when Israel was conquered and carried into exile, the nations reasoned that Israel's God was like the gods of the other nations, limited in power and unable to deliver His people. This event will set the record straight.

Finally, as in chapter thirty six, we hear God saying, *I have poured out my Spirit upon the house of Israel,* a very key statement and one that indicates clearly that Israel will experience a spiritual rebirth and great spiritual vitality. But note the context in which this statement is made – it is the context of God's great intervention on the part of Israel against the Northern/Islamic invasion described in chapters thirty eight and thirty nine.

With that background, let us proceed to examine those crucial chapters.

CHAPTER SEVEN: The Northern / Islamic Invasion

For some reason it has been difficult for Bible scholars to pinpoint an exact time for this conflict. They have suggested times as far removed as "sometime before the Rapture" (Cooper) to the end of the Millennium (those who identify this passage with Revelation 20:8). The present writer believes that there are good reasons for rejecting both of those extremes.

First, the biblical teaching of imminency would be nullified if we made some event prophetically necessary before the Rapture could occur. No matter what is said, if some event must happen before Christ returns for the Church, then He cannot come at any moment as the Bible clearly teaches, but His coming must await that event. This then is definitely untenable!

As far as the suggestion that this is the same battle as the one referenced as Gog and Magog in Revelation 20:8, the use of the words in the Revelation text is not at all like the reference in Ezekiel 38-39. The reference in Ezekiel is precise with the obvious intent of being taken literally. The reference in Revelation is general and is used only as an expression indicating "hordes of people," rather than specific nations. Dr. Dwight Pentecost lists five reasons why this could not possibly be the same event, which for lack of space we cannot reproduce here but suffice to say, there is good reason to reject this view. 22

Having said that, it is important that we establish the time frame in which the events of chapters thirty eight and thirty nine will occur. In point of fact, this should not cause us any difficulty because the text itself gives us the answer and in a very straightforward manner. Take a look at the phrases listed below, gleaned from chapter thirty eight.

- *After many days thou shalt be visited:* (vs. 8)
- *in the latter years thou shalt come into the land that is brought back from the sword, and is gathered out of many people* (vs. 8)
- *. . .upon the people that are gathered out of the nations, which have gotten cattle and goods, that dwell in the midst of the land* (vs.12)
- *In that day when my people of Israel dwell safely* (vs. 14)
- *it shall be in the latter days* (vs. 16)

So the answer very clearly is, This is going to take place in the latter (or last) days. However the next question is, "The latter days of what?" – Or perhaps more precisely, "Whose latter days?"

The Old Testament phrase, *latter days* is somewhat akin to the phrase, *the last days* as used by New Testament writers and in the later context it often refers to the last days of the Church Age. For instance, that is how Paul uses it when he says, *In the last days perilous times shall come . . .* (2 Timothy 3:1). Here Paul apparently means the last, or latter days of this present Church Age. But the last days of the Church Age and the last days of Israel's prophetic calendar are two entirely different time periods.

Israel's prophetic calendar was revealed to the prophet Daniel and recorded in the ninth chapter of the book that bears his name. In it, God told Daniel that seventy weeks or **shabua** (a Hebrew word that simply means "a seven") were determined upon his people Israel. It quickly becomes obvious upon closer scrutiny that Daniel was not to understand mere periods of seven days, but rather seventy sets of seven years. Hence the entire period of time God set to finish His testing of Israel would be 490 years.

Daniel marks the beginning of the countdown at the going forth of a commandment to restore and to build Jerusalem which had been destroyed in 586 BC. The historical date of that decree is one of the best established dates of history. It was March 14, 445 B.C. On that date, Artaxerxes issued a decree to Nehemiah (see Nehemiah 2:1 – 8), for the express purpose of allowing the city of Jerusalem to be rebuilt. The beginning of Daniel's time period then is dated from that decree.

Daniel's prophetic calendar of 490 years was broken up into three time periods, seven weeks (49 years), three score and two weeks (62 x 7 or 434 years) and one final week (7 years). According to the prophecy, at the end of the first two periods, totaling 483 years, Daniel was told that Messiah would come, and indeed He did, for in exactly 483 prophetic years (a prophetic year always has exactly 360 days x 483 years = 173,880 days) Messiah Yeshua rode triumphantly into the city of Jerusalem on a day known to us as Palm Sunday.

Now Daniel was told that after the 483 years Messiah would be cut off or killed. Yeshua was crucified five days later. Notice that it was not to happen during the 483 years nor was it to happen during the final seven years, but in an indeterminate period of time, a gap or parenthesis, between that first 69 seven-year period and the last seven year period known also as the 70th week.

Right now, that indeterminate time, that parenthesis, has lasted over two thousand years. The entire Church Age, which had been kept a secret in the Old Testament, and which was never perceived by the prophets (Ephesians 3:5), is a parenthesis in Israel's prophetic calendar. Israel, prophetically speaking, cannot begin counting days again until that final seven year period begins.

So what bearing does that have on the question, of the "latter days", or what does the term *latter days* mean when it is applied to Israel? The answer is clearly, *latter days* for Israel must refer to any time within that final seven years of Daniel's prophetic calendar.

We conclude therefore that the events of Ezekiel chapters thirty eight and thirty nine cannot occur until sometime after the beginning of that final seven year period. Further, the Church, the

Body of Christ will be Raptured before that period begins (1 Thessalonians 4:13 – 18). Certain key events are predicted which will mark the beginning of that final seven year period. With all that in mind then, let's narrow things down to a more precise time during that last seven years.

A Covenant With Death

To accomplish the task of determining the timing of this event, we begin by once again looking at Israel's prophetic calendar found in Daniel chapter nine. Daniel 9:27 tells us that the Prince that shall come (who has also been identified as the great one-world leader known as the Beast or Anti-Christ) will confirm a seven year covenant with Israel, which will be the signal that the last week of Daniel's prophecy has begun. Exactly what this covenant consists of we are not told, but references to it are found in a number of places in Scripture.

Isaiah 28:14-20, in its immediate view, predicts the Assyrian captivity of Ephraim (the northern ten tribes are so designated). However, the words of Isaiah go beyond the immediate and local scene and look beyond to another covenant which Isaiah calls *a covenant with death, and an agreement with hell.* Surely these words express the true significance of that seven year covenant with Antichrist.

Doubtless, one of the features of this covenant is the promise of military protection for Israel. There is evidence that before this aggression from the north takes place, Israel will have disarmed and left her defenses in the hands of the one-world leader who will guarantee her safety.

Another feature very probably will be the guarantee of Israel's right of independent religious practice in the midst of a world under the dominion of the false religion of the great whore, Babylon the Great. In any case, what the covenant accomplishes is that it effectively binds Israel to the Antichrist and his government for the next seven years. This is precisely what Jesus predicted when, after the Jews had rejected the kingdom which He offered, He said, *I am come in my Father's name, and ye receive me not: if another shall come in his own name* (the Anti-Christ), *him ye will receive* (John 5:43).

It is this covenant with Antichrist, for religious autonomy and military protection, which signals the beginning of the last Week of Daniel's prophecy, also generally known as the Great Tribulation. This signing of the covenant apparently takes place shortly after the Rapture. Just exactly how long after the Rapture is not certain, but most of the sweeping changes of any new administration take place in as little as one hundred days, and it will likely not require more time than this for the Beast to consolidate his kingdom and put his program into operation.

Please keep in mind that the Rapture is not the starting point of the 70th Week, although the two events are apparently closely related. It is the signing of the covenant between Israel and the Antichrist which marks the beginning of that period (Daniel 9:27).

So based upon all that we have learned, chapter thirty eight indicates that this invasion of Israel will occur sometime after Israel has returned to her land. It will occur during the last seven years of Israel's prophetic calendar in a time known as Daniel's 70th Week, and it will occur (obviously) before the Golden Millennial Age. Since it occurs during the Tribulation (or 70th Week), it must occur after Israel's covenant with the Beast, which we have noted marks the beginning of that period.

Now, we also know that the Beast (or Anti-Christ) himself invades Jerusalem at the middle of the Week setting up an image of himself in the restored temple and proclaiming himself "God" (Daniel 9:27; Matthew 24:15; 2 Thessalonians 2:4). Since he is not in Jerusalem when this battle takes place and not involved in this conflict, it would seem obvious that this invasion must occur sometime during the first three and one half years of that seven year period, probably in the latter portion of that time.

So we would conclude that the last days spoken of in the Ezekiel passage refer to the later part of the first half of the final seven years of Israel's prophetic calendar. With the time period determined, the picture is now drawn and we turn to the text which will introduce us to the players in this conflict.

Drawing the Battle Lines

Now, let's return once again to Ezekiel chapters thirty eight and thirty nine. As we do we will look once again at the five statements that are descriptive of the situation that will exist when this battle takes place.

- *After many days thou shalt be visited:* (vs. 8)
- *in the latter years thou shalt come into the land that is brought back from the sword, and is gathered out of many people* (vs. 8)
- *. . .upon the people that are gathered out of the nations, which have gotten cattle and goods, that dwell in the midst of the land* (vs.12)
- *In that day when my people of Israel dwell safely* (vs. 14)
- *it shall be in the latter days* (vs. 16)

The prophecy as given to Ezekiel anticipates a very long time between when it was originally given and when it would be fulfilled. It would be, *After many days. . . in the latter years.* We have already determined that the time period is sometime midway during the final week of Israel's prophetic calendar.

Israel is characterized in these words, *brought back from the sword and gathered out of many people.* She is also said to be *gathered out of the nations.* All of these are certainly descriptive of Israel as we see her in the Land today.

In addition Israel is said to have *gotten cattle and goods, that dwell in the midst of the land.* In other words, this returned nation has become wealthy and prosperous. Israel is one of the few countries of the world that is not facing some kind of financial crisis.

The final statement, however, is certainly not descriptive of Israel at this present time; *In that day when my people of Israel dwell safely.* Israel has been anything but safe having gone through at least six major wars (*War of Independence   1948; Sinai War1956; Six-Day War 1967; Yom Kippur War1973;   Lebanon War1982; Grapes of Wrath War1996*), in addition to continual attacks, skirmishes, and bombings.   Israel has been anything but "safe".

This last statement then, presupposes that something has taken place that has made Israel feel secure; so secure in fact that she is later described in this same chapter as the land of *unwalled villages; I will go to them that are at rest, that dwell safely, all of them dwelling without walls, and having neither bars nor gates* (Ezekiel 38:11).

Obviously the words used to describe her defenseless condition are those that would have been familiar to the prophet.   We must remember that these words were written at another time long before modern warfare was known.   But the point the prophet makes is clear enough – Israel will have dropped her guard and made herself dependent on another – the one who made the covenant with her, i.e., the Anti-Christ.   Is it any wonder that Isaiah calls this covenant, *a covenant with death, and an agreement with hell*?

The Identity of These Nations
Now let's turn our attention to the combatants in the conflict. From time to time, names on the world map change. We have lived in a century that perhaps has seen more changes than any other similar period in the earth's entire history. Ten years ago, I hung a missionary map on the wall of my office so that I could trace the locations of our missionary prayer family at their stations throughout the world. Two years ago, I gave up and got a new map. So many countries had changed names and boundaries in the last ten years that it became almost impossible to find anything for which I was looking.

It is not surprising, therefore, that the names used by Biblical writers for certain peoples are often different from those used today. The real challenge is simply to endeavor to trace the name back to its historical usage and try to discover what people it refers to. This is the primary problem in dealing with the passage before us. When this is solved, all other considerations will be plain from the text. So, using the best information we have at hand:

Gog: This word simply means, "head" or "chief ruler," according to Smith Bible Dictionary and every source I have checked.

Magog: is the land over which Gog rules. Josephus, the Jewish historian says, "Magog founded those that from him were called Magogites, but who are by the Greeks were called Scythians"24 "Historically speaking, the Scythians (Magogites) must have immigrated northward in very early times. Historians agree that the Magogites were divided into two distinct races, one Japhetic (or European), the other Turanian (or Asiatic). The Japhetic race comprised those whom the Greeks and Romans called Sarmatians, but who in modern time, are called Slavs or Russians" 25

The Chief Prince: This phrase in the Hebrew is one word – "Rosh." Jesenius Hebrew Lexicon says, "Rosh was the tribe dwelling in the area of the Volga (river). The Scythians who settled in that part of the world were called 'Rosh' by the Orientals and Arabians." Hyman Appleman, a Jewish evangelist who was born and raised in Russia, concurs that the word "Rosh" with the rough breathing is still used to designate Russia until this day. Pentecost quotes Kelly as saying, "the context fixes "Rosh" as a proper name."26

Mescheh and Tubal: Dr. Sale Harrison writes, ". . . Russia was called Muscovy until Ivan the Terrible. He was the first to assume the title, Czar of Russia. Muscovy is a name derived from Mesheck . . ."27

Writing on the word, Tubal, Dr. Harrison says, "The Greek spelling for 'Meshech' and 'Tubal' are 'Mosoch' and 'Thobol.' . . . Without doubt the original Greek names `Mosoch' and 'Thobol' are identical with Moscow and Tobolsk, the capitals of Western and Eastern Russia respectively, the change being entirely accounted for by the pronunciation and spelling peculiar to Russia." Pentecost quotes Gesenius as saying, "Moscow bespeaks Russia in Europe, and Tobolsk bespeaks Russia in Asia."28

It is a matter of interest that this is not some new interpretation of these words for the sake of sensationalism. The etymology of these words appeared over two hundred years ago in the writings of Bishop Lowther of England, and Josephus can hardly be called recent. Philologically speaking, there can be no reasonable doubt concerning these renderings.

Persia: There is no problem here. This nation is one of the Islamic states and changed its name to Iran as recently as 1932. Unquestionably, however, a larger segment of the Islamic peoples are meant than those who presently live in the modern Iran. Nevertheless, modern Iran is one of the chief enemies of Israel and one of the most dangerous.

Ethiopia: The word in the original here is **Cush**. While **Cush** does sometimes refer to Ethiopia, it more likely refers to that part of the country lying just west of the present Ethiopia, namely North Sudan. It would not be likely that modern Ethiopia would be part of this alliance unless she were to come under Moslem control which does not seem to be imminent. **Cush** referring to northern Sudan would be in line with the rest of the confederacy listed here which are almost all Islamic nations.

Libya: According to Compton's Encyclopedia, "Libya was the ancient Greek name for all North Africa."29 If this is indeed the meaning here, then Libya includes the rest of the Islamic Arab states which stretch across North Africa.

Gomer, and all his bands: According to Gibbons, Gomer can be identified as Germany.30 The oldest maps of Europe list Germany as Gomeria. Arno Gaebelein calls the identification of Gomer as Germany, "an established fact." Since Gomer refers to Germany, then *all his bands* must certainly refer to other Germanic peoples, many of which are to be found in the former satellite nations which had been controlled by the Soviet Union before its breakup.

Togarmah of the north quarters: This is the most difficult one to pinpoint. Sale Harrison says, "Jewish writers usually called the Turks Togarmah." Bauman thinks that much more is included,

"Togarmah and all his hordes. . . can scarcely be other than the great Siberian tribes that stretch along the north of Asia to the Pacific Ocean" 31 If so, it would include present day Kazakhstan, Uzbekistan, Turkmenistan, Tajikistan, and Azerbaijan. It should be noted that all of these countries along with those mentioned along North Africa have one thing in common – they are all Moslem / Islamic nations.

Why The Invasion Takes Place
Ezekiel tells us the reason for Gog's designs on Palestine:

> To *take a spoil, and to take a prey; to turn thine hand upon the desolate places that are now inhabited, and upon the people that are gathered out of the nations, which have gotten cattle and goods, that dwell in the midst of the land.* (Ezekiel 38:12)

What does Israel have that these nations want?

Israel's Wealth: As of 2012, Israel ranks 16th among 187 nations on the UN's Human Development Index, which places it in the category of "Very Highly Developed". The Israeli economy withstood the late-2000s recession, registering positive GDP growth in 2009 and ending the decade with an unemployment rate lower than that of many western countries. Behind this economic resilience is the fact that the country is a net lender rather than a borrower nation. 32

Oil: Moses predicted that Israel would one day return to her land and *suck. . . oil out of the flinty rock* (Deuteronomy 32:13). Israel now has a 1,000-mile pipeline from Haifa to Aqaba, pumping 300,000 barrels of the world's finest oil each day.

Bromine: This chemical, used in the production of synthetics, is found in great quantity in the Dead Sea. So is potash and salt. Geologists now estimate the wealth of the Dead Sea at over two trillion dollars (write it $2,000,000,000,000.00).

The Suez Canal: This most important route from the Mediterranean has long been strategic. Whoever controls it controls everything which moves. While Israel does not directly control the canal, she has demonstrated that she is powerful enough to take control if need be in a crisis.

But this is not all. Verse twelve further says, *to take a prey; to turn thine hand upon the desolate places that are now inhabited, and upon the people that are gathered out of the nations, . . . that dwell in the midst of the land.*

If we look again at the list of the nations that will come against Israel in this conflict, we will see that a considerable number of them have already, at this present time, sworn to annihilate Israel and wipe her off the map. Islam held sway over the Land during the years when the caliphates ruled. To Muslims, it is a disgrace on the name of Allah for any non-Muslim peoples to inhabit land that was formerly occupied by Muslims. Hence, it is a religious duty to destroy Israel and drive every last Jew, and every other non-Muslim from that Land. This will be a battle to accomplish that end. There will be no prisoners taken, no quarter given.

Having studied the great unconditional covenants which God made with Israel, we should be well aware of the necessity for the continuance of the nation of Israel in order that God's covenants and promises might be fulfilled. It has always been, therefore, a part of the program and aim of Satan to destroy this people. Those who have attempted the genocide of the Jewish race have included Egypt's Pharaoh (Exodus 1:16 - 22), Persia's Haman (Esther 7:3-4), and Germany's Hitler. Russia consistently persecuted Israel through their pogroms of extermination. The Islamic nations have sworn to completely eradicate Israel. In this battle all of these nations will again fall prey to the same wicked design of the devil and become his tool in a desperate attempt to destroy Israel altogether.

An Outline of the Battle

> *And the word of the LORD came unto me, saying,*
> *Son of man, set thy face against Gog, the land of*
> *Magog, the chief prince of Meshech and Tubal, and*
> *prophesy against him.* (Ezekiel 38:1, 2)

The first thing we notice is that this entire prophecy is made "against" Gog and all his host. We expect then that the end results will be disastrous for Gog. The second thing we notice is that it is God Himself who will muster this battle: *And I will turn thee back, and put hooks into thy jaws, and I will bring thee forth, and all thine army . . . and many people with thee.* (vs. 6)

In fact He does more than muster the battle. Keil & Delitzsch translate that phrase; *I will mislead thee, and will put rings in thy jaws, and lead thee out, and all thine army. . .* The commentary further explains; "to cause to turn away, to lead away from the right road or goal. . . i.e., to mislead or seduce, in the sense of enticing to a dangerous enterprise; Gog is represented as an unmanageable beast, which is compelled to follow its leader and the thought is thereby expressed, that Gog is compelled to obey the power of God against his will." 32

> *. . . horses and horsemen, all of them clothed with*
> *all sorts of armour, even a great company with*
> *bucklers and shields, all of them handling swords: .*
> *. . all of them with shield and helmet: Be thou*
> *prepared, and prepare for thyself, thou, and all thy*
> *company that are assembled unto thee, and be thou*
> *a guard unto them* (Ezekiel 38:6, 7).

Not surprisingly, there are those who stumble over the descriptions of the kinds of weaponry said to be employed here. Such is certainly not what we are accustomed to in our present day with our super high-tech fighting equipment. This fact has led some to insist that this entire prophecy has already taken place in some obscure past. Of course, the problem is that no such battle as is described here has any historic precedent. So are these weapons to be taken literally, or are we simply to understand that this army is equipped with the best military armament available? I cannot answer that question dogmatically, nor do I think it is the central issue of the passage, but I would strongly suppose the later.

Some have asked how modern weapons could be burned as is described in verse nine, since they are primarily constructed of steel? Again, I cannot answer, but perhaps we should remind ourselves that ancient swords, shields, body armor and chariots were also of steel, so perhaps the question remains either way. There are just some things that require faith and this is perhaps one of them. The fact that the clean-up of this battle will extend into the Millennium will be addressed later in our study.

Of this we can be sure, Gog will lead this great alliance of peoples and nations to the battle. The effect of this massive invasion is described in verses eight through sixteen.

> *After many days thou shalt be visited: in the latter years thou shalt come into the land that is brought back from the sword, and is gathered out of many people, against the mountains of Israel, which have been always waste: but it is brought forth out of the nations, and they shall dwell safely all of them. Thou shalt ascend and come like a storm, thou shalt be like a cloud to cover the land, thou, and all thy bands, and many people with thee.* (Ezekiel 38:8, 9)

> *. . thou shalt come from thy place out of the north parts, thou, and many people with thee . . . a great company, and a mighty army: And thou shalt come up against my people of Israel, as a cloud to cover the land;* (Ezekiel 38:14 – 16)

This passage is particularly significant in its description of the multitudes of people who will be involved in this invasion. Words such as, *like a storm,* and, *like a cloud to cover the land,* all suggest an almost innumerable multitude. In fact, I am convinced that is why the writer in the book of Revelation, in attempting to characterize the size of the army of rebels that revolt against the King Himself at the close of the Millennium, uses the language, *Gog and Magog the number of whom is as the sand of the sea* (Revelation 20:8). Those words are not specific in that passage, but meant to describe an unimaginable multitude. The writer is saying, just as when God and Magog invaded Israel the numbers where beyond count, so it will be in this final revolt.

We conclude then that this will be an army unprecedented in its size and one that Joel will describe in these words: *as the morning spread upon the mountains: a great people and a strong; there hath not been ever the like, neither shall be any more after it, even to the years of many generations* (Joel 2:2).

It appears from these next verses that perhaps the initial move was not directly against Israel to begin with, but rather simply into that region. The actual occasion seems to be a movement on the part of the king of the south (Daniel 11:40) to invade Israel. This action is immediately augmented and aided by the northern and Islamic confederacy. However, whatever the initial motive, a thought comes that this is the time to destroy Israel forever.

> *Thus saith the Lord GOD; It shall also come to pass, that at the same time shall things come into thy mind, and thou shalt think an evil thought: And thou shalt say, I will go up to the land of unwalled villages; I will go to them that are at rest, that dwell safely, all of them dwelling without walls, and having neither bars nor gates, To take a spoil, and to take a prey; to turn thine hand upon the desolate places that are now inhabited, and upon the people that are gathered out of the nations, which have gotten cattle and goods, that dwell in the midst of the land* (Ezekiel 38:10 – 12).

A Protest Note
An alliance of nations, not affiliated with Gog and his hordes files a protest note in verse thirteen. The nations mentioned are ***Sheba, Dedan, and Tarshish***. Sheba was the name of a kingdom along the

southern shores of the Red Sea, probably synonymous with present day Yemen though once a part of the Ethiopian Empire. The ancient capital of Saudi Arabia is still called Dedan on many maps today. If so, it would mean that Saudi Arabia, was siding against the nations that were invading Israel. That is not too unthinkable when one realizes that even today, Saudi Arabia is so fearful of her chief enemy Iran, that she has actually encouraged Israel to strike Iran before that nation can develop a full scale nuclear capacity.

> *Sheba, and Dedan, and the merchants of Tarshish, with all the young lions thereof, shall say unto thee, Art thou come to take a spoil? hast thou gathered thy company to take a prey? to carry away silver and gold, to take away cattle and goods, to take a great spoil?* (Ezekiel 38:13)

Tarshish is the most difficult to clearly define. Tarshish is an ancient Phoenician name given to any place where smelting of ore was done. It is used as a general reference to countries to the west, including as far west as Spain and Great Britain. The Phoenicians sailed as far north as England for tin, a metal used in the making of bronze and other alloys, which leads some to connect Tarshish with England.

It may be that the name Britannia is actually derived from a Phoenician word meaning "source of tin." If so, this reference could be to Great Britain making the "lions" (KJV) or "villages"(NIV) of Tarshish Great Britain's colonies, of which the US is most prominent today. The fact that the lion is a symbol of the British Empire may lend support to this view. In any case this seems to be a weakly worded challenge to Gog's intentions, not unlike some of the "protest notes" delivered in our day by member nations to the United Nations over real or perceived injustices. It is obvious here that the protest was a mere symbolic jesture, having zero effect on the aggressors.

In the next verses Jehovah reiterates once again the timing and the fact that His own hand is bringing all of this to pass. Notice, there were more than one of the prophets, as we shall see, who foresaw this catastrophic event. God allowed the wicked ambitions and hatreds of these nations to drive them to a colossal attempt to destroy Israel altogether and in so doing to play right into His hand of judgment. They have revealed what was in their hearts and they have transgressed against the people of God's Covenants and God is angry. In anthropomorphic terms, His fury comes up in His face.

> *. . . it shall be in the latter days, and I will bring thee against my land, that the heathen may know me, when I shall be sanctified in thee, O Gog, before their eyes. Thus saith the Lord GOD; Art thou he of whom I have spoken in old time by my servants the prophets of Israel, which prophesied in those days many years that I would bring thee against them? And it shall come to pass at the same time when Gog shall come against the land of Israel, saith the Lord GOD, that my fury shall come up in my face. For in my jealousy and in the fire of my wrath have I spoken* (Ezekiel 38:16 – 19).

What happens when God gets angry? History should have answered that question for any who would take the time to inquire. Remember what He did to Pharaoh when He *looked through the cloud*, and His anger was kindled at a monarch who had ten chances to repent, yet persisted in attempting to destroy Israel? He took off Pharaoh's chariot wheels and filled his army with terror until they fled in panic and then bringing the sea upon them He destroyed them all. *It is a fearful thing to fall into the hands of the Living God* (Hebrews 10:31).

The Psalmist reflected upon the same thing when he wrote, *Thou, even thou, art to be feared: and who may stand in thy sight when once thou art angry* (Psalm 76:7)? If indeed as Job tells us, *the fear of the Lord, that is wisdom; and to depart from evil is understanding* (Job 28:28), then to attempt to defy God is the epitome of folly. Nevertheless, that is the path Gog and his alliance will choose to follow and their fate will be very similar to that of Pharaoh and a host of others who have attempted a similar course of madness. Ezekiel describes in detail what follows:

> *Surely in that day there shall be a great shaking in the land of Israel; So that the fishes of the sea, and the fowls of the heaven, and the beasts of the field, and all creeping things that creep upon the earth, and all the men that are upon the face of the earth, shall shake at my presence, and the mountains shall be thrown down, and the steep places shall fall, and every wall shall fall to the ground* (Ezekiel 38:19b, 20).

If words have meaning, and we have learned by experience that God's words certainly do, this is not an earthquake for which there is any previous precedence. Note carefully the description of this event:

- The "shaking" of the earth will begin in Israel, a land bridge that is well known for seismic activity. Note however, that this is called *a great shaking*. The Hebrew word is ***Gaw-dole*** which denotes "exceeding to the highest degree." And what is that degree? This tremor is experienced by the *fishes of the sea*. In other words, it creates a subterranean turbulence that will result in what we call a tsunami. The destructive impact of tsunamis can be enormous and they can affect entire ocean basins. The 2004 Indian Ocean tsunami was among the deadliest natural disasters in human history with over 230,000 people killed in 14 countries bordering the Indian Ocean.

- Ezekiel next describes the effect upon the birds. One might ask, how can an earthquake effect birds? This is a most unusual phenomena but not an unknown one. In February of 2014 a meteorological tsunami hit Praia do Cassino beach in Brazil. According to UNESCO a meteorological tsunami (or meteotsunami) is a tsunami-like phenomenon generated by meteorological, or atmospheric disturbances that are often accompanied by gales, typhoons, hurricanes and other atmospheric phenomena.33   So this event combines all of these tramatic conditions and acts even upon creatures in the atmosphere.

- Next please note that while this begins in Israel, it is not confined to Israel but is rather a world-wide event: *the beasts of the field, and all creeping things that creep upon the earth, and all the men that are upon the face of the earth, shall shake at my presence.* This is unprecedented.   There have been thousands of earthquakes through the ages, but nothing compared to this. The entire earth shutters. If Ezekiel were alone in pre-seeing this event, that would be enough to assure us of its certainty – but he is not! We will trace evidence in both the Old and New Testaments that confirm Ezekiel's prediction and see that each time, these phenomena are in conjunction with the accompanying events of this passage. It is enough for us here to note that this is a seminal event in human history – there has never been anything like it.

- Lastly we look at the phenomenal damage which this event produces and we hear God saying, *and the mountains shall be thrown down, and the steep places shall fall, and every wall shall fall to the ground.* The mountains are shaken and geographic features are changed.   The Hebrew word is **haw-ras** meaning to destroy, tear down, and it is a word of action – the action of one thing upon another. It is certain that there has not been a seismic disturbance of this magnitude since the days of Noah. The face of the entire earth will feel the effects and be changed.

Now having examined what Ezekiel tells us, what effect will all of that have on this invading army? To say that it will create panic in the ranks would be a gross understatement. Ezekiel describes it like this:

And I will call for a sword against him throughout all my mountains, saith the Lord GOD: every man's sword shall be against his brother. And I will plead against him with pestilence and with blood; and I will rain upon him, and upon his bands, and upon the many people that are with him, an overflowing rain, and great hailstones, fire, and brimstone. Thus will I magnify myself, and sanctify myself; and I will be known in the eyes of many nations, and they shall know that I am the LORD (Ezekiel 38:19b – 23).

The first effect describes the utter chaos and confusion that will grip the armies that have overflowed Israel. The sheer terror and impulse for survival will cause every man to attempt to save his own life and in doing so, view every other man as an enemy to his survival. Thus, *every man's sword shall be against his brother,* and the armies will, as they did in the days of Jehoshaphat (2 Chronicles 20:23, 24) begin to slay one another.

Secondly, God Himself fights against the armies with the weapons of the heavens, *an overflowing rain, and great hailstones, fire, and brimstone.* Whether this is a direct act of God or the result of the trauma caused by the earthquake and its accompanying phenomena, is difficult to say, but whatever the direct cause, God is behind this just as He was in the days of Joshua, when more enemies where destroyed by hail than by the sword (Joshua 10:11).

The final verses of chapter thirty eight make clear the motivation behind all of this. God's name, that is His reputation, has been besmirched badly by Israel's performance both while they were in the Land and after their dispersion. That is the subject at the opening of Chapter thirty six beginning at verse sixteen. God allowed Israel to go through their suffering because of their repeated and persistent disobedience and sin, but the nations reasoned that Israel's God was simply not able to defend them. To the nations looking on, Israel's defeat was Jehovah's defeat. Jehovah intends to change that perception.

So the miracles He is about to do for Israel are not based on any good in Israel iself, but on the two fold impetus of (1) the covenants made with the fathers, and (2) the restoration of God's reputation among the nations. God will fulfill the covenant promises and God will work on Israel's behalf so marvelously that *it shall no more be said, The LORD liveth, that brought up the children of Israel out of the land of Egypt; But, The LORD liveth, that brought up the children of Israel from the land of the north, and from all the lands whither he had driven them: and I will bring them again into their land that I gave unto their fathers* (Jeremiah 16:14, 15).

Then, as if that were not enough, God will bring all of Israel's most aggressive enemies against them at one time in an armed alliance the like of which the world has never seen; and when they have overflowed the mountains of Israel, God will bring such destruction upon them that all former miraculous interventions will seem small. Jehovah will demonstrate in the most decisive way possible that He is the sovereign God and no nation, or nations can successfully oppose Him or resist His will. God will restore His reputation among the heathen. The words of the Psalmist take on new meaning:

> *God is our refuge and strength, a very present help in trouble. Therefore will not we fear, though the earth be removed, and though the mountains be carried into the midst of the sea; Though the waters thereof roar and be troubled, though the mountains shake with the swelling thereof. Selah. There is a river, the streams whereof shall make glad the city of God, the holy place of the tabernacles of the most High. God is in the midst of her; she shall not be moved: God shall help her, and that right early. The heathen raged, the kingdoms were moved: he uttered his voice, the earth melted. The LORD of hosts is with us; the God of Jacob is our refuge. Selah. Come, behold the works of the LORD, what desolations he hath made in the earth. He maketh wars to cease unto*

the end of the earth; he breaketh the bow, and
cutteth the spear in sunder; he burneth the chariot
in the fire. Be still, and know that I am God: I will
be exalted among the heathen, I will be exalted in
the earth. The LORD of hosts is with us; the God
of Jacob is our refuge. Selah. (Psalm 46:1 – 11)

While these verses have a direct application to the battle of Armageddon which will be yet future to this battle, they express beautifully the way in which God will get honor to Himself through this event. We see the effect this event has had on the nations that attacked Israel, and we can imagine the effect it might have on the nations that stood by and allowed it to happen. But what effect will it have on Israel? That is the key question and the one we will attempt to answer in the next chapter.

CHAPTER EIGHT: The Results and Aftermath of the Invasion for Israel & Islam

The Effects Upon Gog and His Islamic Allies

We will consider first the opening words of chapter thirty nine:

> *Therefore, thou son of man, prophesy against Gog, and say, Thus saith the Lord GOD; Behold, I am against thee, O Gog, the chief prince of Meshech and Tubal: And I will turn thee back, and leave but the sixth part of thee, and will cause thee to come up from the north parts, and will bring thee upon the mountains of Israel: And I will smite thy bow out of thy left hand, and will cause thine arrows to fall out of thy right hand. Thou shalt fall upon the mountains of Israel, thou, and all thy bands, and the people that is with thee: I will give thee unto the ravenous birds of every sort, and to the beasts of the field to be devoured. Thou shalt fall upon the open field: for I have spoken it, saith the Lord GOD. And I will send a fire on Magog, and among them that dwell carelessly in the isles: and they shall know that I am the LORD* (Ezekiel 39:1 – 6).

The wording here is a repeat of that in chapter thirty eight verses one through four with certain specific additions. Both passages pronounce God's judgment in bringing these nations together against Israel, but chapter thirty nine tallies the results. There will be only about one sixth (16 out of 100), of Gog's hordes that will survive to return to their homeland. God will fight against them as He did in the days of the Judges. The scene here seems reminiscent of the battle with Sisera (Judges 4). In that instance God drew the armies of Sisera to the river Kishon (Judges 4:7), for the very purpose of destroying them. In the Song of Deborah and Barak found in Judges chapter five we read:

> *The kings came and fought, then fought the kings of Canaan in Taanach by the waters of Megiddo; they took no gain of money* (i.e., the armies took no spoil). *They fought from heaven; the stars in their courses fought against Sisera* (a poetic way of saying God intervened through all the forces of nature). *The river of Kishon swept them away, that ancient river, the river Kishon. O my soul, thou hast trodden down strength. Then were the horsehoofs broken by the means of the pransings, the pransings of their mighty ones.* (Judges 5:19 – 22)

The song celebrated the victory of God over the might of Sisera. In the midst of the battle God sent a sudden downpour of water and a torrent swept across the dry riverbed and destroyed Sisera's army. In a similar, but much more dramatic fashion, God will destroy this invading army from the north. In this instance God makes their weapons useless; *I will smite thy bow out of thy left hand, and will cause thine arrows to fall out of thy right hand* (Ezekiel 39:3). They will be slain by the combined forces of nature and the panic that will cause them to slay one another.

This innumerable host of northern powers and Islamic nations will fall on the mountains of Israel. It is ironic, that they wanted the Land for themselves, and God says He will give them a place in it – to be buried in; *it shall come to pass in that day, that I will give unto Gog a place there of graves in Israel* (Ezekiel 39:11). Furthermore the number of the dead will be so great that it will take seven months to bury them (Ezekiel 39:12), and the carrion birds and beasts of the fields will feed upon their carcasses.

And, thou son of man, thus saith the Lord GOD;
Speak unto every feathered fowl, and to every
beast of the field, Assemble yourselves, and come;
gather yourselves on every side to my sacrifice
that I do sacrifice for you, even a great sacrifice
upon the mountains of Israel, that ye may eat
flesh, and drink blood. Ye shall eat the flesh of the
mighty, and drink the blood of the princes of the
earth, of rams, of lambs, and of goats, of bullocks,
all of them fatlings of Bashan. And ye shall eat fat
till ye be full, and drink blood till ye be drunken,
of my sacrifice which I have sacrificed for you.
Thus ye shall be filled at my table with horses and
chariots, with mighty men, and with all men of
war, saith the Lord GOD (Ezekiel 39:17 – 20).

Finally, God further says, *And I will send a fire on Magog, and among them that dwell carelessly in the isles: and they shall know that I am the LORD.* (Ezekiel 39:6). The Bible Knowledge Commentary says, "God will also punish the homelands of the invaders: . . . Sending fire implies destruction and military devastation." Just what is meant is not entirely clear, but could it be that while the armies of Gog and his allies are being destroyed on the mountains of Israel, opposing countries are retaliating with a nuclear attack on Gog's own land? I don't know, but in some way, just as Gog and his Islamic cohorts have thought to destroy the Land so God now destroys their land. The phrase, *in the isles,* is to be understood as follows: "The nation that will spawn the invasion will herself be destroyed. The "isles" (KJV) or "coastlands," already mentioned several times by Ezekiel (cf. Ezekiel 26:15, 18; 27:3, 6-7, 15, 35), imply bordering nations to Gog." 34

The picture that immerges from this event is the near total destruction of the northern powers and all of Israel's Islamic enemies. Their armies lie dead upon the mountains of Israel, and their nations are devastated by fire. Suddenly, with one act, God has removed the threat of Islam from both Israel and the world. It is now Allah who is disgraced and his satanic disguise has been removed. He is seen for the non-god that he is, the ancient Destroyer who comes but to steal and to kill and to destroy. The force of Islam is gone, and her credibility is broken.

Perhaps this helps explain the apparent absence of Islam in prophecies of later events. It also may explain the restoration of Israel's ancient temple worship as clearly predicted in other prophecies. This central and seminal event appears to accomplish the situation necessary for the total power of the Beast and the fulfillment of the remaining prophecies of Daniel's 70th week.

The Further Effect Upon the Nations

That the traumatic effect upon Gog and his allies and their homelands will be devastating none can deny; but there is another result which God had in mind. The nations had concluded that Israel's God was just too impotent to defend His people and now Jehovah will demonstrate His awesome power on their behalf. No reasonable man can deny that what has taken place looks very much like a Divine intervention. Both Israel, and the nations must see the evidence. Here is the outcome:

> *And I will set my glory among the heathen, and all the heathen shall see my judgment that I have executed, and my hand that I have laid upon them. . .And the heathen shall know that the house of Israel went into captivity for their iniquity: because they trespassed against me, therefore hid I my face from them, and gave them into the hand of their enemies: so fell they all by the sword. According to their uncleanness and according to their transgressions have I done unto them, and hid my face from them* (Ezekiel 39:21 – 24).

Just as the nations of old heard how God had destroyed Egypt, the mightiest empire in the world of that time, and drowned Pharaoh's army in the Red Sea and just as they trembled at the Name of this mighty God, so now the nations must once again consider what God has wrought and fear before Him. The Psalmist said it well;

Come, behold the works of the LORD, what desolations he hath made in the earth (Psalm 46:8).

The nations must also realize that Israel's suffering was God's discipline upon His people because Jehovah is not only a God of power, but He is a God of justice and holiness. So God accomplished another of the objectives set forth back in chapter thirty six – the restoration of His glory as the just and sovereign God over the affairs of men. There is in addition, an even more profound result.

The Profound Effects Upon Israel
The events of these chapters will have a momentous effect upon the nations, but they will have an even more profound effect upon Israel. Several things will happen.

First, God's name will be revered as never before among the Jewish nation. The nation that Ezekiel had described in chapter thirty seven as a valley of dry bones has come together: *there was a noise, and behold a shaking, and the bones came together, bone to his bone. And when I beheld, lo, the sinews and the flesh came up upon them, and the skin covered them above: but there was no breath in them* (Ezekiel 37:7, 8), and is about to be transformed. Israel was assembled as a nation but had no *breath in them,* that is, no spiritual life, but something happens as a result of this invasion that will change all of that. Ezekiel describes it in the following verses:

> *So will I make my holy name known in the midst of my people Israel; and I will not let them pollute my holy name any more: and the heathen shall know that I am the LORD, the Holy One in Israel* (Ezekiel 39:7).

> *So the house of Israel shall know that I am the LORD their God from that day and forward* (Ezekiel 39:22).

Then shall they know that I am the LORD their God . . . Neither will I hide my face any more from them: for I have poured out my spirit upon the house of Israel, saith the Lord GOD (Ezekiel 39:28, 29).

If words have meaning, then it is impossible to miss the point – God intends to use this event to bring spiritual life to Israel. Two very specific things drive us to that conclusion. First is the fact that the house of Israel (that is the nation), will know God in a way that they have not known Him heretofore. Israel has existed, and does so today, in a state of separation from God, for Jesus' words are still true, *No man cometh unto the Father but by me* (John 14:6).

Many Israelis are complete secularists – that is, they do not believe that God even exists. Others have a vague idea of God but are more concerned with the traditions of their religion than with God Himself. Few – very few really study the Scriptures themselves. Most rely upon the rabbis for whatever understanding of God they might have. Ezekiel tells us that at this time all that will change. The house of Israel will come to "know God."

Of course the second significant thing that indicates certainly this is what is meant is the further statement: *I have poured out my spirit upon the house of Israel, saith the Lord GOD* (Ezekiel 39:29). The ancient promise of the pouring out of God's Spirit upon His people Israel is now fulfilled. Israel, or the greater part thereof, are born of God. It is this concept Jesus discussed with Nicodemus and rebuked him for his ignorance of what that meant. Remember His words, *"Jesus answered and said unto him, Art thou a master of Israel, and knowest not these things* (John 3:10)? And how could Nicodemus have known them? Because right here in these four chapters of Ezekiel God gives an unmistakable picture of the need of the new birth, and the process of the new birth. Without it Israel is a corpse, with all his parts, but spiritually dead. That is the picture of the nation today – reunited, a national entity, but for the most part a nation without God and without Christ.

The Spirit blows upon this corpse and Israel is given life. So said our Lord Himself; *The wind bloweth where it listeth, and thou hearest the sound thereof, but canst not tell whence it cometh, and whither it goeth: so is every one that is born of the Spirit.* (John 3:8). God spoke to Israel through Ezekiel;

> *Behold, I will cause breath to enter into you, and ye shall live: And I will lay sinews upon you, and will bring up flesh upon you, and cover you with skin, and put breath in you, and ye shall live; and ye shall know that I am the LORD. . . So I prophesied as I was commanded: and as I prophesied, there was a noise, and behold a shaking, and the bones came together, bone to his bone. And when I beheld, lo, the sinews and the flesh came up upon them, and the skin covered them above: but there was no breath in them. . . Then said he unto me, Prophesy unto the wind, prophesy, son of man, and say to the wind, Thus saith the Lord GOD; Come from the four winds, O breath, and breathe upon these slain, that they may live. So I prophesied as he commanded me, and the breath came into them, and they lived, and stood up upon their feet, an exceeding great army.*
> (Ezekiel 37:5 – 10)

Jesus told Nicodemus that he should have understood the New Birth and the role of the Spirit in producing it. Was Jesus being fair? Was there really a legitimate expectation that the "teacher of Israel" (Nicodemus), should have understood the necessity and process of the New Birth? The answer is, "Yes," precisely because God had both predicted it, defined it, and illustrated it here in Ezekiel.

Let me reiterate; (1) Chapter thirty six declares that God will both restore the nation Israel and bring them to know Him. (2) Chapter thirty seven describes that happening with the vision of the valley of dry bones and the two sticks that become one in Ezekiel's hand.

(3) Chapters thirty eight and thirty nine define the events that will surround the miracle of dry bones becoming a mighty spiritual army. In short, Ezekiel's primary focus in these chapters is the future spiritual conversion of Israel. Along with that comes the destruction of her fiercest enemies, the collapse of the Islamic powers and a whole new balance of power in the world.

CHAPTER NINE: The Same Prophetic Picture from the Other Prophets

God seldom reveals a great truth without giving it through the voice of two or three witnesses. What He has promised and predicted in one place, He will repeat and expand in another. That principle is so firmly established that if the student misunderstands and/or misinterprets a passage he can be corrected or confirmed by other Scripture. That is certainly the case in the subject before us.

We have already seen that both the Old and the New Testaments predict a future spiritual conversion for Israel. We have heard the concerted voices of the prophets echoing the same theme. Now we have seen how God has revealed through Ezekiel the time and circumstances of that event. Can we now find a collaboration of what Ezekiel has said in any of the other prophets? The answer is, I believe we can.

The Prophecy of Joel
Anyone who has ever tried to understand the prophecy of Joel, knows that there are interpretational problems. In the first place, we know little about who Joel is. In fact, we know only the name of his father. We do not know his tribe or the location from which he wrote. Furthermore, we do not know the time of writing, thus we do not know what immediate event or actual invasion Joel may have referenced. There are however, some things we do know.

We know that there had been an invasion of locusts that had devastated the Land as it had never been devastated before. One commentator says of this event, "Nothing in the experience of Joel's generation or that of their ancestors was able to match the magnitude of this recent locust plague. The unique event would be spoken of throughout coming generations" 35

Locusts were understood to be a judgment from God, with the purpose of bringing His people to repentance. God had brought such a plague upon Pharaoh during the time of the Exodus in an attempt to bring the monarch to repentance. Solomon, as he prayed his prayer of dedication for the temple says,

> *If there be dearth in the land, if there be pestilence, if there be blasting, or mildew, locusts, or caterpillars; if their enemies besiege them in the cities of their land; whatsoever sore or whatsoever sickness there be: Then what prayer or what supplication soever shall be made of any man, or of all thy people Israel, when every one shall know his own sore and his own grief, and shall spread forth his hands in this house: Then hear thou from heaven thy dwelling place, and forgive, and render unto every man according unto all his ways, whose heart thou knowest; (for thou only knowest the hearts of the children of men:) That they may fear thee, to walk in thy ways, so long as they live in the land which thou gavest unto our fathers* (2 Chronicles 6:28 – 31).

Always, the presence of such plagues was a sign to Israel that God was calling them to repentance. Now Joel sees this invasion of locusts and in his vision they become an invading army so vast, so devastating, and so pervasive that the entire Land is destroyed before them.

Whether Joel's vision had an immediate reference to the Assyrian or the Babylonian invasion of Israel we do not know. But whatever the immediate circumstance may have been the spirit of prophecy frequently sees both a near and a future view of the same event. In this case there can be little doubt that Joel foresaw an invasion in Israel's future that would take place in the last days.

We can be absolutely certain that Joel's vision looks far into the future because much of the phenomena that is said to accompany this invasion never took place in any past invasion and has never taken place to this day. I believe that will become more evident as we proceed to look at the text.

The uniqueness of the locust invasion is in clear view in the opening verses of the book:

> *The word of the LORD that came to Joel the son of Pethuel. Hear this, ye old men, and give ear, all ye inhabitants of the land. Hath this been in your days, or even in the days of your fathers? Tell ye your children of it, and let your children tell their children, and their children another generation. That which the palmerworm hath left hath the locust eaten; and that which the locust hath left hath the cankerworm eaten; and that which the cankerworm hath left hath the caterpillar eaten* (Joel 1:1 – 4).

This invasion of locusts was unlike any other in memory and was an event that would be recited to future generations. The totality of the devastation they wrecked upon the Land is described in verse four.

Joel pointed out the obvious – this tragedy is from Jehovah and it is His call to His people to repent and turn to Him. Joel says, *Sanctify ye a fast, call a solemn assembly, gather the elders and all the inhabitants of the land into the house of the LORD your God, and cry unto the LORD* (Joel 1:14).

However, even as Joel speaks of that invasion of insects, his words go beyond and see another invasion taking place. We get a glimpse of it in the following verses:

For a nation is come up upon my land, strong, and without number, whose teeth are the teeth of a lion, and he hath the cheek teeth of a great lion (Joel 1:6).

Blow ye the trumpet in Zion, and sound an alarm in my holy mountain: let all the inhabitants of the land tremble: for the day of the LORD cometh, for it is nigh at hand; A day of darkness and of gloominess, a day of clouds and of thick darkness, as the morning spread upon the mountains: a great people and a strong; there hath not been ever the like, neither shall be any more after it, even to the years of many generations. A fire devoureth before them; and behind them a flame burneth: the land is as the garden of Eden before them, and behind them a desolate wilderness; yea, and nothing shall escape them. The appearance of them is as the appearance of horses; and as horsemen, so shall they run. Like the noise of chariots on the tops of mountains shall they leap, like the noise of a flame of fire that devoureth the stubble, as a strong people set in battle array. Before their face the people shall be much pained: all faces shall gather blackness. They shall run like mighty men; they shall climb the wall like men of war; and they shall march every one on his ways, and they shall not break their ranks: Neither shall one thrust another; they shall walk every one in his path: and when they fall upon the sword, they shall not be wounded. They shall run to and fro in the city; they shall run upon the wall, they shall climb up upon the houses; they shall enter in at the windows like a thief (Joel 2:1 – 9).

The interplay here between the invasion of the locusts and that of the actual army is subtle and sometimes difficult to distinguish. The locusts are like an army and the army is like locusts. In either case the cause and result are the same. God has brought them as a call to repentance and the devastation they leave behind them is total.

Zuck in the Bible Knowledge Commentary concludes the following as regards Joel's prophecy, "Joel's prophecy deals with Israel's future apart from the chronological gaps which one sees so readily in retrospect. Consequently prophecies pertaining to his own generation are merged here with those that await future realization." 36

Although the "army" involved is nowhere named or precisely identified, it cannot be without significance that we read in verse twenty, *I will remove far off from you the northern army.* While the identification is not decisive, it does fit nicely into the picture we have just examined in Ezekiel thirty eight and thirty nine. But is it the same event? There will be other indicators that will help us determine that.

The cry and description of Israel's response is found in both chapter one and two:

> *Gird yourselves, and lament, ye priests: howl, ye ministers of the altar: come, lie all night in sackcloth, ye ministers of my God: for the meat offering and the drink offering is withholden from the house of your God* (Joel 1:13).

The first invitation to repentance in chapter two comes from God Himself:

> *Therefore also now, saith the LORD, turn ye even to me with all your heart, and with fasting, and with weeping, and with mourning: And rend your heart, and not your garments, and turn unto the LORD your God: for he is gracious and merciful, slow to anger, and of great kindness, and repenteth him of the evil. Who knoweth if he will return and repent, and leave a blessing behind*

*him; even a meat offering and a drink offering
unto the LORD your God* (Joel 2:12 – 14)?

Then comes the call from the leaders in Israel. Notice the basis of their plea – why should the heathen rule over them or say, "where is their God?" The later being the very thing the heathen said when Israel was carried away captive. Jehovah's name, and Jehovah's reputation is at stake.

Blow the trumpet in Zion, sanctify a fast, call a solemn assembly: Gather the people, sanctify the congregation, assemble the elders, gather the children, and those that suck the breasts: let the bridegroom go forth of his chamber, and the bride out of her closet. Let the priests, the ministers of the LORD, weep between the porch and the altar, and let them say, Spare thy people, O LORD, and give not thine heritage to reproach, that the heathen should rule over them: wherefore should they say among the people, Where is their God (Joel 2:15 – 17)?

The tremendous response of the nation to this situation is in itself unique. If indeed, as we believe, Joel is foreseeing the coming great northern invasion of the end time described by Ezekiel – if indeed they both are seeing one event, then perhaps there is an explanation for Israel's sense of helplessness and outcry to God.

Some years ago I remember reading a quote from General Moshe Dayan, (the then very well known general who lead Israel to victory and returned them to the Temple Mount in 1967). Dayan was questioned by a reporter about Israel's readiness in the face of renewed Arab threats. I cannot forget his words. He said, "With the Arabs we shall always be able to do – but if Russia attacks us, all would be lost."

I remember that quote, even though I cannot account for it, because it has always provided an insight for me into Israel's psychic. Israel can rely on its own strength to fight its battles with the Arabs. But there is something deep within their very soul that tells them that they would be helpless before the forces of a combined Arab / Russian advance. If that is true today when Israel is strong militarily, how much more would it be true if Israel had given up its military protection to another? That will apparently be their condition after signing the covenant with the Anti-Christ. In such a situation, Israel would have no recourse but to cry out to God. Strange how much that situation mirrors that of Jacob, the first Israel, who laid hold of God in his helpless desperation facing an approaching army.

We come next to the response of Jehovah to their pleas. Notice, these words are not dissimilar to those we read in Ezekiel.

> *The earth shall quake before them; the heavens shall tremble: the sun and the moon shall be dark, and the stars shall withdraw their shining: And the LORD shall utter his voice before his army: for his camp is very great: for he is strong that executeth his word: for the day of the LORD is great and very terrible; and who can abide it* (Joel 2:10, 11)?

> *Then will the LORD be jealous for his land, and pity his people* (Joel 2:18).

The response of Jehovah is to come to the aid of His people and there are indications of both natural and supernatural phenomena that will accompany that rescue. Look at the results as regards the "northern army."

> *But I will remove far off from you the northern army, and will drive him into a land barren and desolate, with his face toward the east sea, and his hinder part toward the utmost sea, and his stink shall come up, and his ill savour shall come up, because he hath done great things. Fear not, O land; be glad and rejoice: for the LORD will do great things* (Joel 2:20, 21).

Although these words may be a little less graphic than those used by Ezekiel, the similarities are unmistakable. These armies will be removed – the word implies they will be removed violently. Many will be killed, for Joel here reflects upon the putrefying stench which will come from their dead bodies. Ezekiel had said, *I will give unto Gog a place there of graves in Israel, the valley of the passengers on the east of the sea: and it shall stop the noses of the passengers: and there shall they bury Gog and all his multitude* (Ezekiel 39:11). The similarities are too numerous to miss.

There is one final thing which convinces me that we are dealing with the same event. As Joel concludes this event he says, *And ye shall know that I am in the midst of Israel, and that I am the LORD your God, and none else: and my people shall never be ashamed* (Joel 2:27). This is significant. It speaks, I believe of spiritual renewal. And if this were all that Joel said, I would strongly suspect that he was talking of the same set of circumstances and the same responses as we saw in our study of Ezekiel. But Joel does not stop there. Rather it is in this very context, of an enormous invasion from the north and of God's miraculous and dramatic deliverance, that Joel writes:

> *And it shall come to pass afterward, that I will pour out my spirit upon all flesh; and your sons and your daughters shall prophesy, your old men shall dream dreams, your young men shall see visions: And also upon the servants and upon the handmaids in those days will I pour out my spirit. And I will shew wonders in the heavens and in the earth, blood, and fire, and pillars of smoke. The sun shall be turned into darkness, and the moon into blood, before the great and the terrible day of the LORD come. And it shall come to pass, that whosoever shall call on the name of the LORD shall be delivered: for in mount Zion and in Jerusalem shall be deliverance, as the LORD hath said, and in the remnant whom the LORD shall call* (Joel 2:28 – 32).

Now no Bible student can read those words without immediately remembering that they are the very words quoted by the Apostle Peter on the Day of Pentecost when God poured out His Spirit and the Church was born. Peter used Joel's prophecy to explain what was taking place in the pouring out of the Spirit, but the attending phenomena so prominent in the prophecy was not seen at that time. No, and in fact, subsequent events would show that Israel did not repent on a national level and that while Pentecost mirrored to some extent what Joel foresaw, it did not provide the fulfillment of it.

Without a doubt, Joel looks forward to the end time and Israel's final days. In the third chapter he foresees another invasion, not this time from a northern army, but from the armies of the world. Joel's third chapter foresees the battle of Armageddon. But in chapters one and two, Joel deals with that earlier event, the invasion from the north, and just as Ezekiel, Joel sees the outcome as Israel being brought to spiritual conversion and becoming a force for God in the earth.

So we have at least two places where we can trace this sequence. Taking the two passages together we can discern the following:

1. Israel will be restored to her homeland.
2. At some point she will enter into a covenant with the coming world leader, the Anti-Christ.
3. Israel will surrender her military protection to that leader under the terms of the covenant.
4. Israel will know a brief period of peace and apparent safety.
5. An alliance including Russia, parts of Germany and many of the Islamic nations will sweep down upon Israel like a cloud (or like a swarm of locusts).
6. The attack will be initially successful and much of Israel will be destroyed.
7. In the midst of their helpless situation Israel will cry out to God in repentance.

8. God will answer with a mighty deliverance that will involve a world wide earthquake and other catastrophic natural phenomena.
9. The invading armies will be destroyed by a combination of natural catastrophes and human panic.
10. Israel will experience conversion on the part of an unprecedented number of its people.

In our next chapter, I want to examine whether there is still another place where Scripture brings these events together. I believe we will discover that there is.

CHAPTER TEN: The Testimony of the Book of Revelation

In spite of what many think, there is an amazing amount of agreement between writers of Premillennial persuasion on the future prophetic events that concern Israel and the nations, and while they may vary on certain details they are agreed on the basic facts.

One of those things upon which there is general agreement is that there will be an abundant harvest of souls from every nation during the terrible days we refer to as the Great Tribulation. It would be hard to miss that fact in the face of the plan testimony of Scripture:

> *After this I beheld, and, lo, a great multitude, which no man could number, of all nations, and kindreds, and people, and tongues, stood before the throne, and before the Lamb, clothed with white robes, and palms in their hands; And cried with a loud voice, saying, Salvation to our God which sitteth upon the throne, and unto the Lamb. And all the angels stood round about the throne, and about the elders and the four beasts, and fell before the throne on their faces, and worshipped God, Saying, Amen: Blessing, and glory, and wisdom, and thanksgiving, and honour, and power, and might, be unto our God for ever and ever. Amen. And one of the elders answered, saying unto me, What are these which are arrayed in white robes? and whence came they?*

And I said unto him, Sir, thou knowest. And he said to me, These are they which came out of great tribulation, and have washed their robes, and made them white in the blood of the Lamb (Revelation 7:9 – 14).

This glorious sight is certainly in contrast to the terror and horror of the period itself and a cause for tremendous rejoicing, knowing that God will continue to extend His grace to all who will receive it, even during that terrible time. The very existence of this great multitude however, raises not just praise, but some obvious questions. How did all these people come to faith in the Lord Jesus Christ and from whom did they hear the message?

Most Premillennial expositors agree that the Rapture of the Church will occur before the Tribulation commences. With the Church in heaven, who is left to carry the message of salvation? Make no mistake that it will still be true that; *Faith cometh by hearing and hearing by the Word of God.* Who then reached this vast multitude and reaped such a fruitful harvest of redeemed souls?

It is not without significance therefore, that the verses that precede this glorious picture speak of the sovereign God choosing twelve thousand out of each of the tribes of Israel and setting a seal upon their foreheads. While hardly any Jew can trace his tribal ancestry and this very fact has been used by some to cast doubt on the literal fulfillment of this passage, God keeps perfect genealogical records and there is no reason to doubt He will accomplish exactly what He has purposed. Remember that Ezekiel prophesied the restoration of all of the twelve tribes (Ezekiel 37:15 -23) and there are no "lost ten tribes" as far as God is concerned.

Furthermore, trying to escape the problems by making these 144,000 merely "spiritual children of Abraham" does not meet the test of rightly dividing the Word of truth. God is capable of both telling us what He intends to do and performing it. There are then, a hundred and forty four thousand Jewish witnesses here, and most believe they will carry the message of the gospel throughout the world, thus producing the tremendous harvest of redeemed souls seen by John in verses nine through fourteen.

While it is true that the text does not state that there is a direct causative relationship between the redeemed out of Israel in Revelation 7:1 – 8, and the innumerable multitude from every tribe and nation in Revelation 7:9 – 14, the proximity of the two groups within the text suggest as much. After the spiritual conversion and commissioning of 144,000 witnesses, the results of their labors seems clearly to be the multitude of redeemed from around the world.

All this would agree with those passages, particularly in Matthew's Gospel, where Christ sends his disciples to preach the "gospel of the kingdom", that is, the good news that the King is coming and the Messianic Kingdom will soon be established. Many expositors agree that passages like Matthew chapter twenty four are addressed to the Jewish remnant of the last days.

Still, that raises another question. If these are converted servants of God out of the tribes of Israel, how and when were they converted? How did they come to the faith they now proclaim to every tribe and tongue and nation?

The scenario is frequently portrayed that Israel is preserved as a nation through the Tribulation and then comes to faith when Christ ascends in clouds of glory at His coming. The favorite verse for this is Zecheriah 12:10, *And I will pour upon the house of David, and upon the inhabitants of Jerusalem, the spirit of grace and of supplications: and they shall look upon me whom they have pierced, and they shall mourn for him, as one mourneth for his only son, and shall be in bitterness for him, as one that is in bitterness for his firstborn.*

This passage does indeed look forward to Christ's second advent when Israel will literally "see" Him and officially recognize Him as their long rejected Messiah and Savior. However, the question is then raised, if Israel does not experience salvation until Christ returns to earth, who proclaims the gospel during the time of the

Tribulation that will result in the multitudes of redeemed spoken of in the passage sited above? Or again, why do these 144,000 sealed individuals appear at or near the middle of the Tribulation Week?

I do not claim to have all the answers to these questions, but several things seem clear. At least 144,000 Jewish persons will be sealed and preserved by God and will subsequently, *follow the Lamb withersoever He goeth* (Revelation 14:4). They are said to be redeemed and to be the *firstfruits unto God and to the Lamb.*

So if they are the firstfruits, that implies that there will be many others to follow. It would appear then that we should expect a particular event that would precipitate the conversion of at least these who represent twelve thousand from each of the tribes of Israel. Let's be clear, 144,000 is not a small number.

In reflecting upon the prophetic events at the time of Christ's return and the response of the nation Israel at that time, I am reminded that Israel's seven annual Feasts as set forth in Leviticus chapter twenty three are both commemorative and prophetic in nature. That is, each of the Feasts looks back to remember and celebrate something in Israel's history, but each also looks forward to anticipate a greater event in the future.

The four spring feasts were all fulfilled prophetically: Passover and Unleavened Bread when Christ died (1 Corinthians 5:7, 8), Firstfruits in Christ's resurrection (1 Corinthians 15:20, 23), and Pentecost at the coming of the Holy Spirit and birth of the church (Acts 2). We have been living, prophetically speaking, in verse twenty two of Leviticus twenty three, the summer season of sowing and reaping (see also Matthew 13).

There are yet three fall Feasts to be fulfilled prophetically. They are the Feast of Trumpets which will call Israel back to the Land for the final time (Matthew 24:31), the Day of Atonement, which is not a "feast day", but rather a "fast," which focuses particularly upon national sin and repentance, and finally, the Feast of Tabernacles, which will be celebrated during the Millennial

Kingdom and celebrates the presence of the King dwelling among His people (Zechariah 14:16).

While Passover, relates to the removal of personal sin by the Passover Lamb, the Day of Atonement is a national event, a day of reflection upon the sins of the nation. I believe it will be fulfilled in the prophetic picture of Zechariah 12:10 – 14. On that day, Israel will nationally repent and acknowledge her Messiah. The nation that cried, *Crucify Him – away with Him, we have no king but Caesar*, will acknowledge Him and weep for their sin.

While that event occurs at Christ's coming, it seems to be more of an official recognition of sin and a time of national repentance, whereas, the events surrounding the invasion from the north, lead to multitudes of individuals coming to Messiah repentance and personal salvation. We do not, therefore, have to assume that Israel's remnant will have to wait until Christ's return for the outpouring of the Spirit and a new birth experience.

There is yet another reason we are looking at this passage in Revelation. We have already noticed the sequential nature of the sealing of the one hundred and forty four thousand and the conversion of the innumerable multitude from every kindred, tribe and nation. But there is, I believe, another sequential relationship that is often overlooked.

We all know that the chapter and verse divisions we find so helpful in our Bibles were not a part of the original text. We have also realized, I'm sure, that those who placed them for us, sometimes interrupted a subject or a reasoned argument, thus actually cutting it in half and making it more difficult to follow the writer to his logical conclusion. In other words, we always need to make sure that we do not stop reading just because a chapter break appears. Read on, at least a few lines, to make sure the author's thought has not been interrupted.

Perhaps that is the reason many have not seemed to notice the connection between the events in Revelation 7 and the closing verses of Revelation six.

And I beheld when he had opened the sixth seal, and, lo, there was a great earthquake; and the sun became black as sackcloth of hair, and the moon became as blood; And the stars of heaven fell unto the earth, even as a fig tree casteth her untimely figs, when she is shaken of a mighty wind. And the heaven departed as a scroll when it is rolled together; and every mountain and island were moved out of their places. And the kings of the earth, and the great men, and the rich men, and the chief captains, and the mighty men, and every bondman, and every free man, hid themselves in the dens and in the rocks of the mountains; And said to the mountains and rocks, Fall on us, and hide us from the face of him that sitteth on the throne, and from the wrath of the Lamb: For the great day of his wrath is come; and who shall be able to stand (Revelation 6:12 – 17)?

The sixth chapter of Revelation gives an overview of the time of trouble as it develops upon the earth. As each seal is opened, the situation becomes ever more intense and severe. As the chapter comes to a close we are approaching the time when the full force of God's intervening judgments will begin to be poured out – that part of the seven years which can correctly be called the *Great Tribulation*. That is the sense of the announcement in verse seventeen.

That would place the events covered in the preceding verses of this chapter at the first half of the seven year period, and that in turn would place the earthquake and attendant phenomena right about the end of that first three and one half years.

We have already examined the scope of the earthquake that occurs as recorded by Ezekiel, and if there is doubt as to the likelihood of a seismic event of this magnitude, one has only to read recent reports of precursive events taking place in our time.

Earthquakes in Diverse Places

"A leading earthquake scientist has warned that the planet could be cracking up after a series of massive quakes in just 48 hours. Expert Gheorghe Mar'mureanu - from Romania's National Institute of Earth Physics - says 39 quakes have hit the globe within two days. (He was making reference to the week of April 11, 2012).

The series started with two massive quakes in Indonesia measuring 8.6 and 8.2 on the Richter scale, rapidly followed by three more only slightly smaller in Mexico within hours. "There is no doubt that something is seriously wrong. There have been too many strong earthquakes," said Marmureanu.

He added: "The quakes are a surprise that cannot be easily explained by current scientific knowledge. With the Indonesian quake for example, statistically, there should be one big earthquake in this part of Asia every 500 years. However, since 2004, there were already three quakes with a magnitude of over 8, which is not normal." 38

Why is all this significant? Because Ezekiel predicted just such a world wide catastrophic quake would occur in the midst of the invasion of Israel by the northern armies (Ezekiel 38:19, 20). There are some unmistakable similarities.

1. Both are global events.
2. Both involve atmospheric disturbances in the heavens.
3. Both topple mountains and structures.
4. Both create terror, confusion, panic and a fear of God.
5. In both cases, this event immediately precedes the spiritual conversion of Israel.

Thus I would argue that in attempting to understand everything that surrounds the conversion of a major portion of the nation of Israel, we need to include Revelation 6:12 – 7:14 in our study. And when we do we see at least three clear indications of Israel's conversion and the events that precipitate and surround it; the earthquake, the sealing of 144,000 and the conversion of a multitude out of the Tribulation era.

Now that leads to another question. If indeed we have a major event with world impact occurring in or around the middle of the seven year period, what effects will all of this have on the very powerful religious and political forces that are in play at that time? What now happens to these newly converted sons of Israel? What about the covenant Israel signed with the Beast or Anti-Christ?

It is now incumbent upon us to move beyond the spiritual conversion of Israel and examine the repercussions of that event on both Israel and the world. We must look at the effects of the total devastation of the Russian and Islamic armies, the realignment of the balance of power and how all of that fits into the remainder of the prophetic picture. All that and more we will attempt to do in the next section.

SECTION THREE:

THE CONSEQUENCES

AND CHALLENGES

OF ISRAEL'S CONVERSION

CHAPTER ELEVEN: The Effects of the Defeat of the Northern Confederacy

The almost total annihilation of the Great Confederacy of Russia and the Islamic Nations will certainly have profound effects on the world scene. There are at least two areas where this change will be immediately felt.

The first will be on the world's political scene. With the removal of the Northern/Islamic power block, the last obstacle in the path of the Beast toward complete world power will be removed. The fact that this great confederacy of nations made up of Russia, Germany and the Islamic nations attacked Israel without the blessing of the Beast makes clear that he had not yet brought the entire world under his dominion. Now, with those powers destroyed, he will move one step closer to total power. Indeed John describes it in these words, *And they worshipped the dragon which gave power unto the beast: and they worshipped the beast, saying, Who is like unto the beast? who is able to make war with him* (Revelation 13:4)? Revelation chapter thirteen describes the Beast's rise to power.

> *And I stood upon the sand of the sea, and saw a beast rise up out of the sea, having seven heads and ten horns, and upon his horns ten crowns, and upon his heads the name of blasphemy. And the beast which I saw was like unto a leopard, and his feet were as the feet of a bear, and his mouth as the mouth of a lion: and the dragon gave him his power, and his seat, and great authority. . . And*

they worshipped the dragon which gave power unto the beast: and they worshipped the beast, saying, Who is like unto the beast? who is able to make war with him?

And there was given unto him a mouth speaking great things and blasphemies; and power was given unto him to continue forty and two months. And he opened his mouth in blasphemy against God, to blaspheme his name, and his tabernacle, and them that dwell in heaven. And it was given unto him to make war with the saints, and to overcome them: and power was given him over all kindreds, and tongues, and nations. And all that dwell upon the earth shall worship him, whose names are not written in the book of life of the Lamb slain from the foundation of the world (Revelation 13:1 – 8).

Now that the great power of the Russian/Islamic confederation has been removed, it appears that the Beast moves at once into Israel with an army of occupation and sweeping changes are instituted. Daniel says, *And he shall plant the tabernacles of his palace between the seas in the glorious holy mountain* (Daniel 11:45a).

Such a move of course, violates the covenant which had been ratified at the beginning of the 70th Week, and which guaranteed Israel's political autonomy and religious freedom. Some justification must, of course, be offered for this audacious act, so the greatest of all lies is forged on the anvil of expediency. What, then is that lie?

To gain credibility the Beast needs a liaison in Israel, who will endorse him and promote him and he finds that partner in the one the Bible calls the Beast out of the earth (literally, out of the Land i.e., the Land of Israel). This individual is also called "the False Prophet," in Revelation 16:13. We read of him in the following verses:

And I beheld another beast coming up out of the earth; and he had two horns like a lamb, and he spake as a dragon. And he exerciseth all the power of the first beast before him, and causeth the earth and them which dwell therein to worship the first beast, whose deadly wound was healed. And he doeth great wonders, so that he maketh fire come down from heaven on the earth in the sight of men (Revelation 13:11 – 13).

When the Beast marches into Palestine and into Jerusalem, the False Prophet will have already organized a group of unbelieving and apostate Jews to meet and receive him. There is evidence to suggest that it was this same individual (although not yet revealed in his character as the False Prophet) that influenced the *many* to accept the covenant with the Beast in the first place (Daniel 9:27).

Now the political ambitions of the Beast will take on a religious character and, with bold effrontery, the False Prophet will declare the Beast to be Israel's Messiah/Savior and the one who delivered them from the Russian/Islamic hordes. In proof of this, the False Prophet is empowered by Satan to do great signs and lying wonders (Matthew 24:24; 2 Thessalonians 2:9-10; Revelation 13:13-14), which exert such a profound influence upon men that they are ready to *worship the beast.*

With such fervency does the world accept this whole charade, that it is called in Scripture *strong delusion* and *the lie.* The world, anxious for someone who will leave them alone in their sin and still deliver them from the consequences of their evil ways, will pant after this deceiver with all the frantic fervor of a worshiper of Baal (1 Kings 18:28), and all the passion of a teenage Beatle fan. So complete will be the acceptance of the Beast, as the "Deliverer" and "World Messiah" (Revelation13:8), that the Prophet will put the final touch to this Great Deception by an act described in the books of both Daniel, Matthew, 2 Thessalonians and Revelation.

It is probably at this time that the Third Temple (or Tribulation Temple) will be built. We know because of other Scripture that a Jewish Temple must exist in order to fulfill the prophecies of Daniel 9:27. In order for that to occur the major obstacle standing in the way of such a project must be removed – that object is the present Dome of the Rock, a chief Islamic shrine which stands upon the former Temple Mount.

Following the war of Ezekiel chapter thirty eight and thirty nine, Islam's threat to Israel will have ended. The hordes of Islam will lie dead upon the mountains of Israel. There will be nothing to prevent the Dome of the Rock from being removed and the Third Temple being built. It is possible, and even likely that the Beast will promote and even participate in that project.

Now remembering that the Beast came to power in league with the apostate religious system of the Harlot (Revelation 17:1-9) and is therefore accepted by the Gentile religious world, and since he is now proclaimed the "Deliverer of Israel", the only thing he lacks to make him thoroughly Messianic is a throne in Jerusalem. It is this which the False Prophet now provides him, when in the most daringly blasphemous act that has ever been committed by angels or man, the Prophet orders an image of the Beast to be set up in the newly constructed Holy of Holies in the Temple at Jerusalem. (Daniel 9:27; Matthew 24:15; 2 Thessalonians 2:3-5; Revelation 13:11-15).

Daniel tells us that this *abomination that maketh desolate* will cause the Jewish worship (sacrifice and oblation) to cease. He tells us further that it will remain until the "culmination" of the Week. Jesus said that it would be set up *in the holy place,* i.e. in the Holy of Holies in the Temple. And to John, it is revealed that so great will be the deception that the image will actually be empowered by Satan to speak. As a result of all of this, the demand goes out from the False Prophet that all of the world should *worship the beast.*

Now it must be evident to any enlightened person that the desire for a unified world religious system is as old as Babylon itself (Genesis 11:4), and that the underlying motive for such a system has been far more political than religious. It is the same today in the so-called Ecumenical movement, which is just another step toward the building of the Mystery Babylon religious system described so vividly in Revelation chapter seventeen. The Beast will support this system for political reasons and so will the *ten kings* that are allied with him (Revelation 17:12-13).

However, when the Beast is proclaimed the world Deliverer and Messiah, and when his image is set up in the Holy of Holies in Jerusalem, apostate Babylon suddenly will become a rival system and a political liability rather than an asset. The true attitude of the kings of the earth toward her is revealed in Revelation17:16. It is the attitude which men have toward any prostitute, that of patronizing disgust.

Now that the desires of these kings have been satisfied, they *hate the whore, and shall make her desolate and naked, and shall eat her flesh, and burn her with fire*. In short, they will totally destroy the one-world apostate religion and wipe her and her priests, her ministers, and her hierarchy from the earth. John tells us that these wicked kings are actually used by God as His instrument to destroy that false system which has deceived the world for so long (Revelation 17:17).

Wreaking God's vengeance upon her, they destroy her forever. She is no longer needed and so men, who have long seen and known her hypocrisy and sham, turn all of the inbred disgust for her into action and destroy her utterly. This action thus makes room for the last unified false religion; *and they give their kingdom unto the beast.*

Revelation 13:8 tells us that the whole unregenerate world will then be united in the degrading debauchery of worshiping the Beast and making him their god. Thus the first evident effect of the great Deception (2 Thessalonians 2:11, 12), is that Mystery Babylon is destroyed and the sole worship of the Beast established in its place.

Two cataclysmic events have now occurred in quick succession. First, the Great Russian/Islamic Confederacy has been destroyed. Along with Russia, the Islamic nations that supported her have met defeat and devastation and are tottering on the brink of complete collapse. Second, the One-World Religious System called *Mystery Babylon the Great* has been destroyed.

Such earth-shattering events must of necessity send tremors through every strata of society, and the next quake is bound to come at the most vulnerable fault in the world's political crust . . . its sliding economic system. Revelation 18:1-19 records the lament of the world over Babylon's fall. Notice that the word *merchant* or *merchandise* appears six times in the chapter and that the entire chapter deals with an economic crisis.

This is easily understandable. Not only has the balance of power shifted now that Russia and the Islamic powers are destroyed, but all of the nations which depended upon her for economic aid are destitute. Beyond that, the fall of religious and economic Babylon has brought the world to the brink of financial disaster. There is practically nothing in which the ecclesiastical powers of this world do not hold heavy vested interests.

With the sudden total and violent collapse of all of this controlled wealth, is it any wonder that the reaction of the world is concern over commercial matters? The power and popular appeal of apostate systems is always their wealth and never their spiritual abilities.

Jesus predicted this crisis in Luke 21:25. The word translated *perplexity* in this verse is the Greek word *Aporia*. It means literally "without a way." It is the opposite of the word *Emporia,* from which we get our word Emporium, meaning a center of trade. So the word *Aporia* means, "without a way to trade." It indicates the total collapse of the world economic structure, with all currency becoming useless and the result being economic chaos with no way out.

The Beast next employs his greatest stroke of genius – a world economic system built upon loyalty to himself. He personally becomes the "way" of exchange.

And he causeth all, both small and great, rich and poor, free and bond, to receive a mark in their right hand, or in their foreheads: and that no man might buy or sell, save he that had the mark, or the name of the beast, or the number of his name (Revelation 13:16-17).

And so, due to the events which we have discussed, the Beast becomes the sole head of a world religion, a political community, and a world system of economy. Could any power be more complete? But there is one fly in this ointment, as we shall see.

Converted Israel

It is difficult to imagine the effects which these great events will have upon a newly converted people. Our study has focused upon how Israel will be brought to faith by the intervention of God upon the occasion of the invasion from the north. Great hosts of Jews are converted to Christ and come to faith.

Immediately, God seals the 144,000 with His seal upon their foreheads (in contrast to the mark of the Beast just noted). These become His witnesses throughout the remainder of the 70th week. Many thousands of others will join them, and many will be slaughtered in the events yet to transpire.

Hardly has Israel recovered from the shock of the invasion and the pouring out of the Spirit upon them, when the Beast marches into Jerusalem and proclaims himself the "Deliverer" and "Savior", and has his image placed in the Holy of Holies in the temple.

We frequently talk of the entire 70th Week as the Great Tribulation, and it is theologically acceptable to do so. But technically, the setting up of the *abomination that maketh desolate* (the image of the Beast, Matthew 24:15-21) signals the actual beginning of what Jesus called, *great tribulation, such as was not since the beginning of the world to this time, no, nor ever shall be.*

With this signal, the believing Jews, so newly come to faith, are warned to *flee into the mountains* (Matthew 24:16), and the last great dispersion of the Jewish people takes place. With this dispersion, the message of the Gospel of the kingdom will be spread throughout the world (Matthew 24:14). The message will, of course, include the Gospel of salvation through Christ, but it will also sound out once again the message of John and of Jesus, *Repent ye: for the kingdom of heaven is at hand.*

The conversion of Israel toward the middle of the Week is the great key to understanding the events of the Tribulation period. Not only does this event throw light on the Tribulation period, but it also opens the riddle of the book of Hosea which we examined in chapter three.

Quickly reiterating what we studied then:

- Hosea is called upon to contract a marriage with a woman who is a harlot. This tragic situation becomes a sign to Israel of her own unfaithfulness to Jehovah, who is Israel's "Husband" (Hosea 1:2).
- Three children are born, but two of them are born of fornication, and Hosea names them appropriately.
- As a result of her repeated acts of unfaithfulness, Hosea declares that she is no longer his wife and he is no longer her husband – he divorces her (Hosea 2:2).
- But at last, Hosea is called upon to go after his faithless wife. She has sold herself to the point where she may now be bargained for on the market. In loving kindness Hosea goes and buys her back (Hosea 3:2).
- He declares that he will "betroth her to himself" once more (i.e. make her his wife again), but this time in faithfulness (Hosea 2:19-20).
- Though he brings her back to himself in love (Hosea 3:1), and at a great price to himself (Hosea 3:2; compare Isaiah 52:3; 53:5-6; 1 Peter 1:18-19), yet he does not permit her to see his face for many days (Hosea 3:3).

What a picture of God's dealing with Israel. The time will come at His Second Advent when Israel will own Him officially as their own and see Him face to face. However, just after their remarkable transformation and conversion, they must abide for Him(i.e., wait for Him), in longing faithfulness, during the many days (1,290 days, Daniel 12:11), or to the end of the Great Tribulation. In that time, Israel will be tried, purified, and made white, and for the first time in her checkered history, she will be found faithful to her Lord (Daniel 12:10).

CHAPTER TWELVE: The Activity of Converted Israel During the Tribulation

In our last chapter, we examined the effect which the events of the middle of the Week will have upon the newly converted remnant of Israel. The entrance of the Beast into Jerusalem, proclaiming himself "Savior" and "Deliverer", and the erection of his image in the Holy of Holies signals to converted Israel the last great exodus from their beloved land.

Jesus had warned them to *flee* (Matthew 24:16), and Hosea tells us that God will provide a path of escape down through the *valley of Achor* (Hosea 2:15). Their escape will be celebrated with singing according to Hosea, *as in the day when she came up out of the land of Egypt* (Exodus 15:1-21).

Where Israel goes from there is difficult to determine. Revelation 12:6, 14 indicates that she fled into the wilderness. Some believe that she will find refuge down in the wilderness of the Sinai Peninsula through which she once wandered for 40 years. Others believe that Daniel 11:41 may indicate that she will take refuge in the wilderness of Petra, the old rock-hewn city of Edom.

But Ezekiel 20:35-36 makes it clear that God's primary reference is not to a literal wilderness, but to that great spiritual wilderness of mankind, called by Ezekiel, *the wilderness of the people.* From her flight down through the valley of Achor, Israel will for one final time be *scattered and peeled* among all nations, only with one vast and important difference.

This time, she will carry with her the message of life eternal through the crucified, risen, and soon coming Savior-King, Jesus Christ. It is through this remnant that *this gospel of the kingdom shall be preached in all the world for a witness unto all nations; and then shall the end come* (Matthew 24:14).

It is in this relation that Isaiah calls Israel, *my witnesses* (read Isaiah 43 and 44). Notice how this title is given in connection with Isaiah 43:2, *When thou passest through the waters, I will be with thee; and through the rivers, they shall not overflow thee: when thou walkest through the fire, thou shalt not be burned; neither shall the flame kindle upon thee.* It is precisely during the deep waters of this Tribulation period that God will at last glorify himself in Israel.

Distinguishing Things that Differ
Before proceeding, there are some very important distinctions we must make. When we speak of *all Israel* being saved, we are speaking scripturally (Romans 11:26), and yet Paul makes it clear that the phrase does not include all of the natural seed of Abraham.

> *For they are not all Israel, which are of Israel: neither, because they are the seed of Abraham, are they all children . . .* (Romans 9:6-7).

Throughout the history of Israel there has always been *a remnant according to the election of grace.* So in the moment of Israel's salvation, not every Jew will be saved, but *all Israel shall be saved,* i.e. every one who is of the spiritual seed of Abraham, a Jew, and one of the elect.

While a vast number of Jews (and presumably the greater part of that nation) will come to faith, there will still be those who resist the Divine revelation and who give their worship to the Beast.

Ezekiel 20:37-38 teaches that Messiah will cause the nation Israel *to pass under the rod,* a phrase that indicates the separation of those who belong to the Shepherd from those who do not, and Ezekiel says, *I will purge out from among you the rebels, and them that transgress against me . . .* So it should be clearly held in mind that when we speak of converted Israel, we do so in the sense that God's elective purposes in grace have been realized and not in the sense that every natural descendant of Abraham has been saved.

There is a strong indication that during the final years of the Great Tribulation, even some who professed faith at the moment of Israel's national conversion will turn back because of the horrors and persecutions that await them. *But he that shall endure unto the end, the same shall be saved* (Matthew 24:13).

The Three Divisions of the Converted Remnant

The Martyred Multitude
The largest group of converted Israel will be those who, during the rigors of the last part of the Tribulation period, will lay down their lives for the sake of the One they so long had rejected.

A number of passages deal with this theme, and all of them are fearful (Deuteronomy 4:30-31; Isaiah 2:19; 13:12-16; 24:1-21; 26:20-21; 43:1-2, 10-13; Jeremiah 30:1-7; Daniel 12:1; Amos 5:18, 20; Zephaniah 1:14-18; Matthew 24:21-22; Luke 21:25-26; and 1 Thessalonians 5:3).

Revelation 13:7 tells us that the Beast was given power *to make war with the saints, and to overcome them.* In Revelation 6:9-11, John is given a vision of a great multitude of martyred saints of this period who will seal their testimony with their blood.

Jesus said, *And except those days should be shortened, there should no flesh be saved: but for the elect's sake those days shall be shortened* (Matthew 24:22). Is it any wonder that John writes as he contemplates this awful time, *Blessed are the dead which die in the Lord from henceforth: Yea, saith the Spirit, that they may rest from their labors; and their works do follow them* (Revelation 14:13). This passage, often quoted at funeral services, has its primary reference to those martyred multitudes that will face all of the diabolical wrath of the Beast and his cadres during the final half of the Tribulation period.

167

What they will have to suffer can only be imagined by contemplating something of the reign of terror during the French Revolution, or something such as the description of the atrocities of Nazi Germany's notorious extermination camps. Such sadistic, brutal murder is satanically inspired and will be repeated with ever increasing frequency as the days of trouble come nearer. It is this that the great multitude of Israel, and those who came to faith in Christ through their witness, will face during their time of trouble.

Beside this direct persecution there will be, economic sanctions applied against any who do not receive the mark of the Beast during this period. They will not be able to buy or sell and many will die of starvation and exposure during that time. It is utterly impossible for words to describe the sufferings of that period. However, for the faithful, eternal triumph is sure, for we read, *they overcame him by the blood of the Lamb, and by the word of their testimony; and they loved not their lives unto the death* (Revelation 12:11).

The 144,000
The second group out of converted Israel will be that band of 12,000 out of each of the twelve tribes of Israel. It is this multitude, though actually quite small in number when compared to the multitudes of earth, that will primarily be used of God during the Tribulation to accomplish the task of worldwide evangelization. Something of the fruits of their efforts is revealed to us in the multitude of redeemed saints that we saw in Revelation 7:9-14.

Some things are said of this group which may seem extreme to us (Revelation 14:4-5), but we must not forget that the days in which they will bear their witness will also be extreme. In view of the intense persecutions of that time, any less spiritual standard would collapse before the storm of satanic pressures. They are accorded a special place of honor before the Throne of God. Notice the following:

- They abstain from all contact with fleshly pleasure for the task before them (Revelation 14:4).

- They follow the Lord Jesus implicitly everywhere He leads them (Revelation 14:4b, compare John 10:27-30).
- They are the firstfruits (Revelation 14:4c), i.e. the first to be redeemed during this period. All others come as a result of their witness.
- They are absolutely honest and walking in the light (Revelation 14:5a, compare 1 Peter 2:1; 1 John 1:5-7).
- They are so sustained by the Spirit of God as to be *without fault* before Him (Revelation 14:5b, compare Jude 24).

The Two Witnesses
In addition to the former two groups, the last group is the smallest of all and perhaps the most potent. They are described in Revelation 11:3-15, and are simply called, *my two witnesses.* Who they are is a subject of sharp debate among students of prophecy. Some believe them to be Elijah and Enoch, the similarities being that both these two prophets were 1) translated, 2) did not see death, and 3) both had a message of judgment (read 1 Kings 17; 2 Kings 2; Hebrews 11:5-6; Jude 14-15).

Others insist that they are Moses and Elijah, since these are the two who appeared on the Mount of Transfiguration (Matthew 17:1-9) and since Satan seems to have had a special interest in the body of Moses (see Jude 9).

Neither view is provable, although many arguments are given. Many are certain that whoever the second man is, the first is Elijah, since his coming is prophesied in the Old Testament (Malachi 4:5).

As regards the second, it cannot be denied that the peculiar features of this last prophet's ministry (i.e. turning water into blood and smiting the earth with plagues) is certainly *much like what* Moses' did. It is a matter upon which each student must be fully persuaded in his own mind. If it were a clear case, so many sincere students would not be divided on the matter. The important thing, however, is what these witnesses accomplished.

The Length of Their Testimony
The message in Revelation makes clear that they testify for a period of 1,260 days, clothed in sackcloth. This is equivalent to 42 months, three and one half years, or a time, times, and half a time. In other words, they prophesy during the latter half of Daniel's 70th Week.

The Character of Their Testimony
They are called two olive trees, which speaks of blessing, and two candlesticks, which speaks of light or testimony. They dress in sackcloth, indicating that their message is one of repentance and judgment (compare 1 Kings 18:21-41).

The Power of Their Testimony
Three things are noted: first, they have power to destroy their enemies. This is unusual power indeed, in that it flows directly from them as it did from Elijah (2 Kings 1). Secondly, they have power over the elements, so that they can bring drought (compare 1 Kings 17:1; James 5:17-18). Finally, they have power to do miracles, turning water into blood and smiting the earth with plagues (compare Exodus 7-11).

The Response to Their Testimony
God promises that He will not leave Himself without a witness and so, even in the devilish times of the Great Tribulation, in the very midst of the blasphemous assumptions of the Beast, in the very city of Jerusalem, God maintains and protects His two witnesses while millions are being martyred all around the globe.

After all is said however, to a people swept away under the strong delusion of *the lie,* their testimony has little effect. In the end, as soon as God removes His protection from them, the Beast displays the real attitude of the world toward these men of God and slays them, leaving their mutilated bodies to rot on the streets of Jerusalem.

Immediately, the word goes out through the news media with television coverage, making a blatant display of their remains (Revelation 11:9). The reaction of the world is a holiday celebration of joy at the death of God's faithful servants.

Having prophesied for the final three and a half years of the Tribulation Week, their bodies now lie in silent witness for three and a half days, when suddenly life from God enters into them and they are raised and taken to glory. It should be noted that this is at the very end of the Tribulation, and the next event is the cataclysmic fanfare of the return of the Lord in glory.

The Effect of Converted Israel upon the Gentile World
We are given in Scripture three indications of the effect of Israel's testimony upon the Gentile world.

As to the extent of their testimony, Matthew 24:14 indicates that in the slightly more than three and a half years after Israel's conversion at the time of the Russian/Islamic invasion, the witnesses of that nation will reach the world with the message of Salvation and the coming Kingdom.

The second indication which we have of the effectiveness of Israel's witness during this period is that vision of the martyred multitude, *of all nations, and kindreds, and people, and tongues* (Revelation 7:9-17). These are distinctly said to be saved, *after this*, or in other words after the conversion and sealing of the 144,000 witnesses of Israel. They are, therefore, very likely the product of their witness.

The unbelievable severity of that time can only be grasped when one realizes that these multitudes have all suffered death during that short period of the Great Tribulation (Revelation 7:14). The worship of any "God" but the Beast will be considered political treason and punishable by death, and the economic sanctions applied against any that refuse the mark of the Beast will slay multitudes with hunger.

It is during this era that the prophetic words of the late George Orwell will know their most complete fulfillment. He wrote, "If you want a picture of the future, imagine a boot, stamping upon a human face. . . forever!" Thankfully, because of Christ intervention at His coming, it will not be forever.

The point here that should be emphasized, however, is that in spite of the terrible character of those days, great hosts of Gentiles will be swept into the kingdom by the testimony of a nation that at long last had brought forth fruit for God. It is precisely as the prophet indicated, *Before she* (Israel) *travailed, she brought forth; before her pain came, she was delivered of a man child* (Christ). The Prophet then continues with a vision of the things we are looking at: S*hall a nation be born at once? for as soon as Zion travailed, she brought forth her children* (Isaiah 66:7-8).

The obvious implication here is that Christ came out of Israel before her time of travail (Great Tribulation), but only as Israel goes into her own time of travail will she finally bring forth fruit for God.

There is yet another group of Gentiles that will be touched by Israel's witness. They may be known as *Ministering Gentiles.* The title comes from Christ's words in Matthew 25:40, *Inasmuch as ye have done it unto one of the least of these my brethren* (the Jews), *ye have done it unto me* (please read Matthew 25:31-46).

The time we see this group is just after our Lord's return. The event is the judgment of the nations. The basis for judgment is the acceptance or rejection of the message of the Gospel which Israel preached during the last awful years of the Great Tribulation. The evidence of acceptance was that they befriended, fed, clothed, protected, and ministered to the scattered remnant of Jews who preached the message to them in those days.

To befriend these, who have been charged with treason by the Beast, will be to incur his wrath and endanger one's life and property. But the evidence of their faith is that they do minister to Israel's messengers, and those who escape are received into the kingdom as true believers.

Dr. Lehman Strauss writes, "The 144,000 witnessing Israelites will be persecuted for their testimony. They will be hungry, thirsty, lonely, in need of clothing, and cast into prison. But those Gentiles who believe their message will stand with them and minister to them, so that it is to them Jesus will say, "Inasmuch as ye have done it unto one of the least of these My brethren, ye have done it unto Me" (Matthew 25:40). This throng will be preserved through the tribulation, not kept out of it as the Church will be (Revelation 3:10)." 39

This assistance to Israel by believing Gentiles during this time is taught in a number of places. Not the least is Revelation 12, where the Great Dragon is seen sending out *a flood* ("an army", see Psalm 18:4; Jeremiah 47:2) after the remnant of Israel, but we read, *that she might fly into the wilderness, into her place, where she is nourished for a time, and times, and half a time, from the face of the serpent.*

Ezekiel 20:35 makes clear that the reference to the wilderness means among the nations. We read that the earth helped the woman. All that is involved here is difficult to say, but the thing that is certain is that Israel will receive help during that period from believing Gentiles who will accept the testimony of the remnant. Many will be martyred for their faith and assistance to the Jews, as we have seen before, but these ministering multitudes will survive.

CHAPTER THIRTEEN: The Last Days Of Gentile World Dominion

And Moses said unto him (Pharaoh), *As soon as I am gone out of the city, I will spread abroad my hands unto the LORD; and the thunder shall cease, neither shall there be any more hail; that thou mayest know how that the earth is the LORD'S* (Exodus 9:29).

The earth is the LORD'S, and the fulness thereof; the world, and they that dwell therein (Psalm 24:1).

> *This is my Father's world,*
> *Oh let me ne'er forget*
> *That tho the wrong seem oft so strong,*
> *God is the Ruler yet.*
> *This is my Father's world:*
> *The battle is not done;*
> *Jesus Who died shall be satisfied,*
> *And earth and heav'n be one. 40*

Thus is joined the great controversy of the ages. Who shall reign over the earth and in the affairs of men? Shall man himself reign with all his humanistic delusions? Or shall Satan, who is the "god of this age and world system," or shall God, through the God-Man, Jesus Christ who is the Eternal Creator and Sustainer of this world and all others. On this planet the contest rages, building through the ages in intensity until in the last years of the 70th Week it reaches its awful climax.

In Revelation chapter five, the Lion of the Tribe of Judah was given the scroll of the title deed to the earth. The remainder of that book tells the story of the battle that ensues as He takes control of what is rightfully His. God had decreed that man should have dominion over the earth and man (Adam) abdicated to Satan by obeying him in the Garden. Now, at long last, the God-Man will come to claim what is His and fulfill the divine decree.

Just how far can sinful man go? That question is posed often today. The answer is that he can go downward until depravity touches reprobation and there is no longer any sensibility left, but being past feeling, man gives himself over to immorality, *to work all uncleanness with greediness* (Ephesians 4:17-19). The big lie of the Antichrist, (along with the delusive signs and wonders of the False Prophet, and the *strong delusion,* which comes as a judgment from God upon those who once rejected the truth), will bring about just such a condition in the final half of the 70th Week.

God Shows His Hand in Judgment -- The Great Plagues
God can no longer allow the blasphemous assumptions of the Beast to go unchallenged, and so He breaks forth upon the kingdom of the Beast with a series of judgments, which are described in the book of Revelation as the Seals, the Trumpets, and the Vials. These great and awful judgments are set forth in the scroll which John saw in Revelation 5:1. According to the description given by the Holy Spirit, this scroll was two sided, *written within and on the back side.*

Personally, I believe that this phrase is the key to understanding the structure of the book of Revelation. The plagues listed throughout the book are not chronological from beginning to end. The Book tells the whole story, but it jumps from one vision to another in order to do so. On the front side of the scroll, the things which John saw upon the breaking of the seven seals were written. Notice that the seven trumpet judgments came out of the seventh seal and are, therefore, part of it. From the opening of the scroll in Revelation 6:1 to the end of chapter 11, there is a sweeping on-rush of events which brings us to the end of the Tribulation and the setting up of Christ's Kingdom (See Revelation 11:15). At this point we are as far chronologically as we are when we reach the end of chapter nineteen.

After the opening of the seventh seal, the scroll is turned over and the other side is read. First, the great actors for good and evil are introduced to us in chapters 12-14. Then there is a partial recapitulation of the events and judgments, described before in chapters 6-11. Compare, for instance, the second vial and the second trumpet judgment, or the third trumpet and the third vial. Compare the sixth trumpet and the sixth vial. I'm sure you see the parallelisms here.

The important thing to remember in studying the plagues is that they are not chronological running from the beginning of the 70th Week until the end, but if carefully examined will be seen to begin in earnest with the opening of the seventh seal and the outpouring of the trumpet judgments, (which the later chapters partially recapitulate). This would indicate that, while the entire period is one of wrath, it is the last half of the Week, following the setting up of the image of the Beast which is particularly characterized by the pouring forth of God's Divine indignation upon rebellious man.

Old Testament Parallels
As we look at the plagues in the book of Revelation, it will be helpful to recall the record of God's controversy with Pharaoh found in Exodus chapters seven through eleven. This passage forms a very strong parallel to the controversy recorded in Revelation between God and the Antichrist. While some of the plagues recorded in Revelation may seem to be couched in symbolic terms, it should be noticed that these in Exodus are extremely literal visitations and they strongly urge a literal interpretation to many (if not all) the plagues of Revelation.

The plagues of Exodus also were spiritual encounters, for *against all of the gods of Egypt I will execute judgment* (Exodus 12:12). Likewise in Revelation, God is pouring out a visitation not only upon the world of rebellious men, but upon the spiritual principalities and powers which have been the real objects of man's worship (Exodus 24:21; 1 Corinthians 10:19-20). The almost inconceivable severity of this period can be sensed when death flees away and wicked man cannot die, and the very atmosphere is filled with unclean and malicious spirits. Satan, himself, comes down in a last desperate effort to overthrow the purposes of God, and nature revolts until the earth is reeling like a drunken man (Isaiah 24:20). It is beyond our ability to totally grasp the horror of those days.

It would be helpful to read, carefully and meditatively, the twenty fourth chapter of Isaiah, allowing the Spirit of God to paint the picture of those final days of Jacob's trouble upon the canvas of the imagination.

> *Behold, the LORD maketh the earth empty, and maketh it waste, and turneth it upside down, and scattereth abroad the inhabitants thereof. And it shall be, as with the people, so with the priest; as with the servant, so with his master; as with the maid, so with her mistress; as with the buyer, so with the seller; as with the lender, so with the borrower; as with the taker of usury, so with the giver of usury to him. The land shall be utterly emptied, and utterly spoiled: for the LORD hath spoken this word. The earth mourneth and fadeth away, the world languisheth and fadeth away, the haughty people of the earth do languish* (come to nothing). *The earth also is defiled under the inhabitants thereof; because they have transgressed the laws, changed the ordinance, broken the everlasting covenant. Therefore hath the curse devoured the earth, and they that dwell therein are desolate: therefore the inhabitants of the earth are burned, and few men left* (Isaiah 24:1 – 6).

Isaiah continues beginning in verse seventeen:

> *Fear, and the pit, and the snare, are upon thee, O inhabitant of the earth. And it shall come to pass,*

that he who fleeth from the noise of the fear shall fall into the pit; and he that cometh up out of the midst of the pit shall be taken in the snare: for the windows from on high are open, and the foundations of the earth do shake. The earth is utterly broken down, the earth is clean dissolved, the earth is moved exceedingly. The earth shall reel to and fro like a drunkard, and shall be removed like a cottage; and the transgression thereof shall be heavy upon it; and it shall fall, and not rise again. And it shall come to pass in that day, that the LORD shall punish the host of the high ones that are on high, and the kings of the earth upon the earth. And they shall be gathered together, as prisoners are gathered in the pit, and shall be shut up in the prison, and after many days shall they be visited. Then the moon shall be confounded, and the sun ashamed, when the LORD of hosts shall reign in mount Zion, and in Jerusalem, and before his ancients gloriously (Isaiah 24:17 – 23).*

Is it any wonder that Jesus said, *except those days should be shortened* (Greek: "cut off," "amputate"), *there should no flesh be saved: but for the elect's sake those days shall be shortened.* (Matthew 24:22)

God's Purpose in the Plagues
In studying the plagues, the purposes of God should be held firmly in mind. At least five purposes are discernable from Scripture.

The plagues have a Dispensational significance. They are a part of the judgment which forms the response of a Holy God to the failure of man during the Sixth Dispensation. Man's response to God's offer of grace through faith was apostasy, the complete rejection of The Faith. The plagues are God's righteous response to the apostasy of the age; they are the inevitable reckoning – God calling man to account – for his failure under the Dispensation of Grace.

The plagues have a consequential significance. They are the evidence of God's governmental dictum, *whatsoever a man soweth, that shall he also reap.* They are the consequence of man's rebellion and failure. Notice how this theme is expressed in such passages as Revelation16:4-7: *And the third angel poured out his vial upon the rivers and fountains of waters; and they became blood. And I heard the angel of the waters say, Thou art righteous, O Lord, which art, and wast, and shalt be, because thou hast judged thus. For they have shed the blood of saints and prophets, and thou hast given them blood to drink; for they are worthy. And I heard another out of the altar say, Even so, Lord God Almighty, true and righteous are thy judgments.* Thus the plagues are the natural consequences of man's behavior.

The plagues have a controversial significance. They are a part of God's controversy with the nations and people which have given their allegiance to the Beast. Like Pharaoh and his cadre of magicians, the Beast and the False Prophet will be shown helpless against the divine judgments of God. They may duplicate, or rather imitate, some of the more minor miracles, but they cannot stop what God is about.

The plagues have a purifying significance. They are a part of the program of God with Israel and are intended by Him to purify Israel from all attachment to this world system and prepare them for His glorious appearing (Zechariah 13:9).

The plagues have a merciful significance. In the plagues is shown forth the mercy of God, in that (1) they are meant to warn man of the consequences of continued sinning, (2) they are intended to bring men to repentance, and (3) they always precede and are less severe than the final judgment, always building in intensity and, therefore, demonstrating the restraint of God in judgment . . . hence that even in judgment He is merciful (2 Peter 3:9-10).

The Last Days of Gentile World Dominion

As pointed out previously, the *times of the Gentiles* will come to an end when Christ reigns from His Throne in Jerusalem as King of Kings and Lord of Lords. What will be the condition of Gentile dominion in those final days of the Tribulation period? Three things may be observed:

Economic Chaos

Frequent reference is made in the book of Revelation to conditions which are indicative of economic chaos and disaster. We have already seen how the destruction of the Northern Alliance, and the fall of the great apostate system of Babylon, left the world in a state of economic collapse. While the Beast immediately instituted his scheme of economy, based on a world economic community with himself as the focal point (the trade symbol being the number of his name, i.e. 666), it cannot be doubted that things soon deteriorate from bad to worse.

Such cataclysmic events, as the total destruction of one third of the vegetation of the earth, and a like number of all of the sea creatures, and a third of all the water on the earth polluted, could hardly lead to anything but the severest kind of famine and privation.

Human Suffering

Under the best of conditions, man is impossibly restive and cannot be satisfied or truly happy. Of course, this is the result of his alienation from God. But how much greater will be his misery when tribulation conditions bring human suffering to a peak of intensity never before experienced in human history. In terms of present population statistics, over three billion people will die in one single trumpet judgment. Grievous sores, scorching sun, poisonous waters, rivers of blood and dead fish, all serve to fan man's bitterness toward each other and God to a raging inferno. *And they gnawed their tongues for pain, and blasphemed the God of heaven . . . and repented not of their deeds.*

Spiritual and Moral Collapse

Revelation 9:20-21 gives something of the picture of the moral and spiritual conditions which will exist during this period. The open worshiping of demons, accompanied by the lowest forms of materialistic idolatry and witchcraft, will be the spiritual order of the day. Men will be plunged into the blackest night of spiritual darkness the world has ever known.

According to the same passage, the moral condition will, as always, follow suit. Murders will be rampant, outrageous sex crimes will be committed, and stealing will become the universal mode of exchange. The unleashed force of demon powers mixed with the unbridled depravity of the human heart will bring the world to a moral and spiritual condition much like the men of Sodom, who were so enflamed by their lust that they continued to grope for the door to sexual gratification after the angel had smitten them with blindness. This is insensible wickedness, and it will be the condition of the Beast worshiping world during the last days (see Micah 7:2-6).

The Orient on the Move

With the deterioration of conditions one great force comes into play which has not occupied our attention before. Lying east of the great Euphrates River is the Orient. From a position of primitive isolation, the nations of the Orient have emerged within this century as world powers to be reckoned with. In the 1940's, the empire of Japan came close to occupying all of the eastern islands, as well as most of China. Although stopped in her mad plan, Japan today has again risen as a world power and is flexing her militaristic muscle.

China has made unprecedented progress toward industrialization and seeks to become the mightiest military power in the world. There can be no doubt that China's ambitions lay to the west.

India has begun to shake herself like a sleeping giant and is now a nuclear power. Within the latter part of the last century, the Orient has come alive industrially, technically, and militarily.

When the northern alliance armies are destroyed upon the mountains of Israel (Ezekiel 38-39) and the Beast moves his army of occupation into Jerusalem and becomes the world's foremost political figure, there must be some temporary infatuation with him among the princes of the east. We are distinctly told that the world will *worship the beast,* which would suggest that, at least initially, they will follow his leadership.

However, as the conditions of the Beast's empire deteriorate, and as the visitations from God fall upon the earth, the kings of the Orient become increasingly disillusioned with this apparent god/man. Revelation 9:13-21 and 16:12-16 both deal with this event.

Forces Behind the Scenes
From a careful reading of these passages, it will be seen that two forces are at work and that they bring about a single result. First, God providentially dries up the river Euphrates, *that the way of the kings of the east might be prepared.* Whether this is to be taken figuratively or literally is a matter of debate. The point is, that whatever obstacles stood in the way of the kings of the east moving their armies westward will be providentially removed by God.

Second, and at the same time, (a) four angels, which are said to be bound in the river Euphrates (and they are therefore wicked angels), are loosed (Revelation 9:14-15). These four angels go forth to incite men to war. Besides this, (b) there are seen *three unclean spirits like frogs come out of the mouth of the dragon, and out of the mouth of the beast, and out of the mouth of the false prophet.* Something is asserted, or some position is taken by this trinity of evil that incites the kings of the east to rebellion. And so, by influences, both Divine and devilish, circumstances are prepared which result in the greatest movement of armies which the world has ever known.

Daniel says of the Beast that *tidings out of the east and out of the north shall trouble him.* With the threat of invasion upon him, the invincible mad man, energized by his master the Dragon, gathers the combined armies of the west together in Palestine to defend his right against these rebels from the east, and from the east, there marches an army of two hundred million (200,000,000) men. If this be thought an incredible figure, contemplate that it is exactly the figure of armed militiamen which are presently estimated to be prepared in China alone.

The text tells us that the opposing forces will include *the kings of the earth and of the whole world* gathered together to battle. Where will it happen? Revelation 16:16 says, *And he gathered them together into a place called in the Hebrew tongue Armageddon.*

Where Is Armageddon?

Dr. Pentecost writes, "The hill of Megiddo, located west of the Jordan River in north central Palestine, some ten miles south of Nazareth and fifteen miles inland from the Mediterranean seacoast, is an extended plain on which many of Israel's battles have been fought. There, Deborah and Barak defeated the Canaanites (Judges 4 and 5). There, Gideon triumphed over the Midianites (Judges 7). There, Saul was slain in the battle with the Philistines (1 Samuel 31:8). There, Ahaziah was slain by Jehu (2 Kings 9:27). And there. Josiah was slain in the invasion by the Egyptians (2 Kings 23:29-30; 2 Chronicles 35:22)." 41

Actually, Armageddon, while referring primarily to the great Plain of Esdraelon (which may be seen by referring to any map of Palestine), has a far larger reference and actually has become synonymous with the last great battle of the nations which will spread over all of Palestine, as various references testify (Isaiah 34; 63; Joel 3; Zechariah 14:2). Joel differentiates between this battle and the invasion of the Northern army which chapter 2 dealt with. The battle of Armageddon, therefore, should be seen as an extended campaign, gathering together the forces of the east and the west at Megiddo, and from there spreading over all of the area of Palestine.

The Outcome of the Battle

The following passages all refer in one way or the other to this event: Psalm 2; Isaiah 10:20-34; 34:1-17; 63:1-6; Daniel 2:34-35, 44-45; Joel 3:1-16: Micah 4:11-13; Habakkuk 3:1-16; Zephaniah 1:14-18; 3:8; Zechariah 14:1-15; Malachi 4:1-3; Matthew 24:7-31; Revelation 14:14-20; 19:1-21. These references taken together present a full picture of the events of that great day insofar as God has been pleased to reveal them to us in His word.

In summary, it can be asserted that the foregoing passages teach:

- The armies of the world will gather themselves together in Palestine upon the great Plain of Megiddo.

- The land of Israel is in dispute, and perhaps all of the Middle East under the authority of the Beast, and this great battle is meant to determine once and for all what will become of him and the Land.

- Sometime during the early stages of the campaign, great destruction is visited upon all of the Land.

- Before the final confrontation of the two great forces can take place, while they are gathered together against each other, *the sign of the Son of man* appears in heaven, and the King of Kings and Lord of Lords rides forth to fight for Israel and to effect His own "final solution" to the dispute of Palestine.

- The kings then turn from fighting one another and combine to fight against Christ and His armies.

- The outcome is certain and the slaughter of a hopelessly wicked world takes place in which such vast hordes die that blood literally erodes the mountains. Confusion and terror grip the armies of earth until they slay one another.

- Upon reaching the earth, our descending Lord stands once more upon the Mount of Olives (from which He ascended 2,000 years ago), and the Mount cleaves in two, from north to south, and a great valley is formed running from east to west. It is into this valley that Christ brings those who remain of the nations for judgment.

That is the summary of the great battle of Armageddon. Too awful to contemplate, it is nevertheless the necessary outcome of man's stubborn refusal to repent and be reconciled to God. Armageddon became a certainty the day Adam rebelled. As in the day of Noah, so in that day there will be no alternative to judgment.

CHAPTER FOURTEEN: Christ's Second Advent and Related Events

The Lord Jesus shall be revealed from heaven with his mighty angels, in flaming fire taking vengeance on them that know not God, and that obey not the gospel of our Lord Jesus Christ: who shall be punished with everlasting destruction from the presence of the Lord, and from the glory of his power; when he shall come to be glorified in his saints, and to be admired in all them that believe (2 Thessalonians 1: 7-10).

In the last chapter, we saw how the armies of the world would be drawn by satanic delusion down to the plain of Megiddo for the great battle of Armageddon. The cup of human iniquity will have come to the full. Human suffering, the natural outcome of sin, will have risen to fever pitch. All hope for universal preservation will be gone. The destruction of natural resources and the complete imbalance of nature will impoverish the world until desperation finds expression in the last great war of the age.

Two hundred million from the Orient and millions more from the west meet together in what would doubtless result in the total annihilation of the race (Matthew 24:22), except that God intervenes. Suddenly in the midst of human chaos, there appears *the sign of the Son of man.* Just what this will be we are not told, but we are told that the world will recognize it and what their reaction toward it will be.

Christ's Second Advent

It is part of the psychology of man that whatever he resents in life, he consciously (or subconsciously) blames on God. Over and over the Bible reveals this fact. Note the reaction of Israel in the wilderness. Moses says, *what are we, that ye murmur against us? . . . your murmurings are not against us, but against the Lord* (Exodus 16:6, 8).

So it has always been. There is a God consciousness in every man, and yet man is alienated from God because of his sin. He, therefore, inwardly blames God for every situation he dislikes. The pitch of human suffering during these final days of Tribulation will be so intense that man will be uncontrollably angry with God. . . . *and they gnawed their tongues for pain, and blasphemed the God of heaven because of their pains and their sores, and repented not of their deeds* (Revelation 16:11).

When *the sign of the Son of man* appears, it brings two immediate reactions. First, it brings a reaction of fury toward God and His Christ, and a desire to strike back at this hated King (Luke19:14, 27). Second, it brings a sense of fear and desperation, for the nations will know that they are fighting for their lives. So, like a beast backed into a corner, frantically and fiercely fighting for its very existence, the mad world will turn from its enmity toward one another and presume to attack the forces of God and His Christ as they descend from heaven.

The picture given by John (Revelation 19) is the most complete. The Coming One is *Faithful and True* (to those who are His), and makes war in *righteousness,* indicating again that, contrary to the present thinking of this world, there is a time to righteously make war. The armies of heaven follow Him. These, we are told by Paul, are heaven's mighty angelic hosts. He is the Lord of heaven's armies (Jehovah Sabaoth), and the outcome of the battle is certain.

While the battle is raging on the plain of Armageddon, another host of elect angels is circling the globe to gather together God's saved ones from the four corners of the earth. This is the final regathering of the elect including the remnant of Israel and is declared in such passages as Isaiah 27:13; Matthew 24:27-31; Jeremiah 31:7-14. With this event, the Old Testament Feast of Trumpets is fulfilled. The remnant is said to be *ready to perish* in the total chaos of a world of cruelty and confusion. Now they are regathered to the camp of Messiah while He destroys their enemies.

The Judgments Associated with the Second Advent

When our Lord's feet stand once more upon the Mount of Olives (Zechariah 14:4), that Mount subsequently divides in two, forming a great valley. The mount will divide from north to south forming a valley which runs from east to west beginning at the eastern gate of Jerusalem.

Interestingly, I remember some years ago being able to detect a fault plain in the Mount of Olives that is visible as one looks toward the mount from the eastern gate. That is the same gate the Moslems walled up and placed a burial ground before it to prevent these very promises from happening. Obviously, they will have no affect on the fulfillment of these prophecies.

The nations of the world will be brought into that valley and Christ will sit in judgment upon them before the same eastern gate. There are at least three separate judgments which will transpire at this time.

The Judgment of the Beast and the False Prophet

In Revelation 19:20, we have one of the most unusual judgments in the Bible. When our Lord returns, the first human individuals with which He will deal will be the ones Scripture calls the beast and the false prophet. This is doubtless because of the extreme wickedness to which they had sold themselves, being completely empowered and controlled by Satan himself. The language here is graphic . . . *And the beast was taken . . .* The Greek word is **piazo** and is translated elsewhere, "lay hands on," "catch," "apprehend," and carries the meaning of an act of force.

Empowered by the Spirit of Darkness, the Antichrist has been able to prevail even against God's two witnesses, but he is no match for the glorified Lord. He is taken by force and the False Prophet with him and *these both were cast alive into a lake of fire burning with brimstone.* When that awful lake is seen again 1,000 years later, these two appear once more, still alive and suffering as its chief victims. Whatever changes in the physical structure of their bodies needs to occur, it evidently takes place here, so that they are not annihilated by that holocaust. The same can be said for all others who go there.

The Judgment of the Nations
By the time this judgment begins, blood will already run deep in the land of Palestine, but the end of the slaughter is not yet. Remember the picture given three times of Christ treading out the winepress of the wrath of God (Isaiah 63:1-6; Revelation 14:14-20; Revelation 19:15). He will not stop until the last drop is wrung from the grapes of wrath.

Revelation 19:21 indicates the next step. Brought into the valley of judgment (Joel 3:9-16; Zechariah 14:4-5), Christ will sit as King of Kings and Lord of Lords to judge the nations (see Matthew 25:31-46). We have already anticipated the basis of that judgment previously when we discussed, "The Ministering Gentiles." Christ will bless those Gentiles who heard and responded to the message of the Gospel preached by the remnant of Israel during the time of Jacob's trouble. These multitudes will show their faith by their good works toward the remnant. They will, therefore, be received into the Millennial Kingdom of Christ, while the others will be judged for not accepting the message. Remember that Israel will have reached the world with the message in just three and one-half years (Matthew 24:14). All will hear, therefore the judgment of the nations will be on the basis of their reception or rejection of Israel's witness to the gospel and the coming Kingdom.

The outcome of the judgment is presented clearly in Scripture. Those who accepted the Gospel preached by the remnant will be ushered into the Kingdom Age (Matthew 25:34). Note that they are saved individuals, as all will be who enter the Kingdom. Those who rejected the message of the remnant and who worshiped the beast will be destroyed with a plague (Zechariah 14:12; Matthew 25:41-46), so that the carrion birds are filled with their flesh (Revelation 19:21). Their bodies will be then disposed of, while their souls descend down to Hades, the place of departed spirits to await the second resurrection and final judgment.

The Judgment of Israel

One final matter still hangs in the balance to be cared for here. The fate of the nation Israel.

What will become of those among Israel who have followed the beast and worshiped his image? Ezekiel tells us, *And I will cause you to pass under the rod, and I will bring you into the bond of the covenant: and I will purge out from among you the rebels, and them that transgress against me: I will bring them forth out of the country where they sojourn, and they shall not enter into the land of Israel: and ye shall know that I am the LORD* (Ezekiel 20:37-38).

Just as the Shepherd of the Nations divided the s*heep* from the g*oats*, so here He will purge out the unbelievers in Israel and their fate (along with all who worshiped the beast) will be as John foretold (Revelation 14:9-12). They will not enter the Land and they will not enter the Kingdom.

On the other hand, the future of the remnant will be glorious. It is this day that will see the complete fulfillment of the Day of Atonement. As pointed out in our study of that day, national sin is dealt with and a nation repents and reverses its official position from one of rejection of Jesus the King (Luke 19:14; John 19:15) to one of officially receiving Him as Messiah, Savior, and King. With this remnant, Christ will fulfill all of the Old Testament covenant promises made to Abraham, Isaac, and David.

It is, therefore, plain from the passages considered here that Christ will judge three distinct groups at His Second Advent. Of course, in addition to these groups, Satan will be taken at this time and bound for a thousand years (Revelation 20:1-3), but this is a temporary measure and his ultimate judgment awaits a future day (Revelation 20:10). Some also believe that fallen angels are judged at this time. We may be sure that they will be judged (1 Corinthians 6:2-3), and Satan's binding must surely be corporate and include all his host as well. One thing is certain, neither Satan or the fallen angels are active during the Millennial reign of Christ.

Resurrections Associated with the Second Advent
Revelation 20:4-5 makes clear that there is a resurrection which is associated with the second advent of Christ. It is called by John, *the first resurrection* (Revelation 20:5). It is at this resurrection that the Old Testament saints are resurrected along with those who were martyred during the Tribulation period.

Throughout both the Old and the New Testaments, the promise of resurrection appears again and again. Job wrote of it (Job 14:13-15) and Isaiah declared it in no uncertain terms (Isaiah 26:19). There can be no justification in spiritualizing these passages. They are obviously meant to be taken in their literal sense and look forward to a time when dead bodies will live again. It should be kept firmly in mind that wherever resurrection is spoken of, it is always in reference to the physical body (except when the word is clearly used in a figurative sense).

Literal resurrection is the coming to life again of a body that has been dead. Whatever the attendant problems of such a doctrine may seem to be, the fact is that the Bible plainly declares that it will happen and faith rests in revelation (Matthew 22:30-31; Luke 14:14; John 5:29; 11:24; Acts 2:31; 4:2; 17:32; 23:6-8; Romans

6:5; 1 Corinthians 15; 2 Timothy 2:18; Hebrews 11:35; 1 Peter 1:3; Revelation 20:5-6).

The Resurrection of Old Testament Saints

Why are we sure Old Testament saints are resurrected at this time? There is some debate among good scholars on this point and so we will examine it briefly here. There are three reasons why we can be sure that Old Testament saints rise here, along with Tribulation saints, and not (as some teach) at the time of the Rapture of the Church. These reasons are:

- Because only those who are *in Christ* are resurrected at the Rapture (1 Thessalonians 4:16). Now certainly Old Testament saints belong to Christ by virtue of His death for them (Romans 3:25; Hebrews 9:15). Christ's death made a propitiation for the sins of all believers of all ages and forms the only basis whereby any can be saved.

  The term *in Christ* is a technical one and refers to that relationship to His Body, which is the product of the baptism of the Holy Spirit (1 Corinthians 12:13). This baptism was never received by any before Pentecost and will never be received again by any after the Rapture. It is this baptism that forms the Body of Christ, the Church of which no Old Testament saint was a member (since the Church did not begin until Pentecost).

  Remember that even John the Baptist, the greatest of Old Testament saints (Matthew 11:11), could only say of himself that he was a *friend of the bridegroom* (John 3:29). Those of us who are saved during this dispensation are members of the Bride. Therefore, Old Testament saints will not be resurrected at the Rapture because, although they belong to Christ (1 Corinthians 15:23), they are not *in Christ*, not being a part of His Body, the Church.

- Because the Scriptures of the Old Testament, which pointed to the resurrection, always associated it with Christ's Second Advent. The key passage is Daniel 12:1-3. Here the sequence of events is clearly set forth. First, the time of trouble (12:1), then the resurrection of the saints (12:2), then the rewarding of the saints (12:3). The resurrection of Old Testament saints clearly takes place after the Tribulation according to this passage.

- Because the Old Testament saints are promised the blessings of the Millennial Age (Isaiah 11-12). Since they must be resurrected to enjoy these blessings, and since this resurrection signifies the last marching order of *the first resurrection,* and since they were not resurrected at the Rapture . . . they will most certainly be resurrected at this time.

The Resurrection of Tribulation Saints
There can be no debate about the time of the resurrection of Tribulation saints. Revelation 20:4 declares in the clearest terms that they who laid down their lives for Christ during the darkest days of the reign of the Beast; *lived and reigned with Christ a thousand years.* Their resurrection therefore takes place here at Christ's second advent.

Final Preparations for the Millennial Age
In Daniel 12, there are three time periods referred to in reference to the events of the Tribulation and the second advent. Each of these time periods dates from the setting up of the Abomination of Desolation (the image of the beast) at Jerusalem.

First there is, *A time, times, and a half a time,* literally three and one half years, or 1,260 days (see Revelation 11:3). This is the period from the Abomination of Desolation to Christ's glorious appearing.

Secondly, Daniel tells us there will be, "1,290 days," and finally, there are "1,335 days."

These periods extend beyond the second advent for a period of 30 days and 75 days respectively. Scofield writes,

"No account is directly given of that which occupies the interval of seventy-five days between the end of the Tribulation and the full blessing of verse 12." It is suggested that the explanation may be found in the prophetic descriptions of the events following the battle of Armageddon (Revelation 16:14; 19:21). The Beast is destroyed, and Gentile world dominion ended, by the smiting of the "Stone cut out without hands" at the end of the 1,260 days, but the scene is, so to speak, filled with the debris of the image which the "wind" must carry away before full blessing comes in (Daniel 2:35). 42

It is apparent then from these references, as well as from another in Daniel 8:14, that there is a definite period of transition which takes place, during which time:

- The judgments and resurrections discussed in this chapter take place.
- Christ consolidates His kingdom and appoints rulers over the nations (Revelation 20:4; 1 Corinthians 6:2; Luke 19:15-19; Matthew 19:27-29).
- The debris of war is cleaned up (see, for example, Ezekiel 39:9, where we learn that there will still be debris left from the invasion of the northern armies).
- The earth is purged from the curse, and Millennial blessedness is established (Romans 8:18-23; Isaiah 11:6-9).
- The temple is cleansed and prepared for Millennial worship (Daniel 8:14).

Obviously, several years are involved here. During this time, Christ will accomplish at least five things with Israel in preparation for His glorious Millennial reign:

- He will regather them out of all countries (Jeremiah 32:37; Ezekiel 11:17; 37:21).
- He will unite them to each other and to Himself (Jeremiah 31:33; 32:38-39; Ezekiel 37:15-20).
- He will restore their sovereignty to them and set King David (whom He will resurrect) over them as their King (Jeremiah 30:8-10).
- He will use Israel to thresh the nations and bring them into subjection (Isaiah 41:13-16; Jeremiah 51:20; Micah 4:11-13), a process that apparently takes longer than is generally recognized.
- He will establish their system of worship and their Temple and reinstate the great Feast of Tabernacles, which will be celebrated in recognition of Christ's sovereignty over all the earth (Zechariah 14:16-19).

Conclusion

We began this study to demonstrate the prophetic destiny of, both Israel and the Islamic Nations. We have observed both the certainty and the circumstances of Israel's future conversion at the invasion of Israel by the Russian and Islamic hordes. We have seen God's miraculous intervention and the destruction of the Russian/Islamic coalition.

We continued to examine some of the consequences and challenges that will come because of and as an outcome of that event. We have seen converted Israel carry the witness of the gospel to the nations of the world. It is the gospel of God's redeeming grace through Jesus Christ and it is also the good news, that the King is coming and the Kingdom is at hand. We have seen something of the results of that message in the numberless multitudes from every nation and kindred and people that are gathered in heaven due to their witness. Remember, these are not the saints of the ages, rather *these are they that have come out of great tribulation and have washed their robes and made them white in the blood of the Lamb* (Revelation 7:14).

In addition we saw a group called the Ministering Gentiles, those who were not martyred, but survived and where gathered with Israel into the Kingdom. They gave witness to their faith by protecting and ministering to the messengers of Israel during the time when all lives were threatened for doing so.

Finally, we peeked into the opening days of the Kingdom age when Messiah will reign, when the ravages of war will be cleaned up, and when the full consolidation of His Millennial Kingdom will begin.

All of that leads us to say in the words of the Holy Spirit; *Behold, he cometh with clouds; and every eye shall see him, and they also which pierced him: and all kindreds of the earth shall wail because of him* (Revelation 1:7).

And so all Israel shall be saved: as it is written, There shall come out of Sion the Deliverer, and shall turn away ungodliness from Jacob: For this is my covenant unto them, when I shall take away their sins (Romans 11:26, 27).

Wherefore God also hath highly exalted him, and given him a name which is above every name: That at the name of Jesus every knee should bow, of things in heaven, and things in earth, and things under the earth; And that every tongue should confess that Jesus Christ is Lord, to the glory of God the Father (Philippians 2:9 – 11).

For those of us who are part of the Bride, we read, *When Christ, who is our life, shall appear, then shall ye also appear with him in glory* (Colossians 3:4).

And finally to you I say, Be certain that you have received Him as your only all-sufficient Savior and Lord now, so that He may own you as His own in the Day of Judgment.

APPENDIXES

APPENDIX ONE:

Abba Eban was Israeli Foreign Affairs Minister, Education Minister, Deputy Prime Minister, and ambassador to the United States and to the United Nations. He was also Vice President of the United Nations General Assembly and President of the Weizmann Institute of Science. He was a master of language, and his speaches were often models of diplomatic agility, but none was ever more so than when he delivered the following:

> *"Never has the Arab nation commanded such elements of freedom, strength and opportunity as those which now lie in its hand. With its twelve Sovereign States, its vast territory, its great resources of manpower and wealth, it has realized ambitions beyond the wildest expectations of recent years.*
>
> *Is the world really asking too much if it demands of this vast empire that it live in peace and harmony with a little State, established in the cradle of its birth, sustaining its life within the narrowest territory in which its national purposes can ever be fulfilled?"* 43

Abba Eban interview 1958

APPENDIX TWO: A Brief History of Early Premillennialism

My purpose in this section, is not to prove Premillennialism, but rather to put to shame the ignorance of those who believe it to be a recent concept without historic precedence and thereby dismiss its claims with indifference.

One of the prevailing myths of our time is that the doctrine of Premillennialism; the teaching of an imminent return of Jesus Christ for the Church, the restoration and conversion of the nation Israel, and the earthly, glorious reign of Jesus Christ over this earth for a thousand years is somehow the late concoction of J.N. Darby (1800 – 1882), and a few of his followers in the nineteenth century.

This idea, this current fable, is so puerile as to deserve no attention at all except for its evident popularity among those who would prefer to brush off the teaching of Premillennialism by scorning it adherents rather than wrestling with its Scriptural and historic foundations. As deceivers in the past have observed, a lie, told often enough evolves into a truth.

While it is true that there was a revival of the study and understanding of the prophetic Scriptures that occurred in increasing regularity in the centuries following the Reformation, that fact does not mean that the insights that began to immerge where new, novel or disconnected to the historically held positions of the church. After all, the Reformation itself was not a movement that created or invented truth, but one which recovered the ancient truth that had been lost through the ages of Roman Catholic imperialism and interpretation.

The Reformation was merely the natural result of the recovery and study of the Scriptures themselves, unencumbered by the barnacles of ecclesiastical interpretation which through the centuries had been encrusted upon them. Once the pure, literal sense of the divine writings was freed from the debris and clutter of human speculation and interpretation, the pure streams of the water of life once more began to flow.

When Luther thundered forth "The Just shall live by faith," it was not some new idea that he had invented, but rather the very foundation of Soteriology as found in the writings of the Prophets, the Apostles and those that followed them. That central truth had been obscured and finally lost by the increments of Rome's creeping heresy that salvation resides in the Church, the Sacraments, and the Priesthood, rather than in the crucified and risen Savior Himself. Luther simply restored the truth that salvation is not earned by a system of infused grace imparted by sacraments and good deeds, but by the imputation of the Divine Righteousness received through faith alone. Luther, and the other reformers, invented nothing – they merely recovered that which had been lost.

Likewise, once the grand truths of redemption were recovered, it was fitting that God should move His people to begin to recover other truths that had been equally buried beneath the debris of Rome's dogma. As some, even among the Reformers themselves, began to study the Scriptures, there was a renewal of interest in those portions of the Word that looked toward things to come – the prophetic Word. This was especially true among early Ana-Baptist leaders, and while some of their conclusions were extreme and proved to be wrong, the desire to understand and accept that part of God's inspired Word was evident.

It is interesting that just as Luther and others returned to the Scriptures and some of the first Century fathers to glean an understanding of Justification by faith, so others began to discover the writings of men like Irenaeus, who was a disciple of Polycarp, who had himself been discipled by the Apostle John who was the penman of the book of Revelation.

Irenaeus had developed a very extensive view of Bible prophecy which he wrote about in his last five chapters of his book, *Against Heresies*. It is further interesting that Irenaeus' book was suppressed and remained hidden throughout the Middle Ages by those who had rejected the Premillennial faith which Irenaeus clearly taught. His book was rediscovered in 1571 and was one of the factors which led to a revival of premillennialism in the early

1600s. Irenaeus' writings played a key role because of their proximity to the Apostles and because of their clear premillennial statements.

I am indebted for the following material to several very helpful sources. As already stated, I have leaned upon **Dr. David Larsen**, Professor Emeritus of Preaching at Trinity Evangelical Divinity School. In his excellent book entitled ***Company of Hope***, he traces the history of the premillennial position from the first Century to the present.

Dr. Thomas Ice in *A Brief History Of Early Premillennialism* was a great help especially in the evidence presented for Premillennialism among the earliest writers. I would refer the reader to:
http://www.pre-trib.org/data/pdf/Ice-ABriefHistoryofEarly.pdf

Finally, the website *Israel Answers* provided additional help especially regarding those who were aware of Israel's future and supported the cause of a return to the ancient Land.
http://www.israelanswers.com/christian_zionism/a_history_of_chri stian_zionism

The Church Historians Testimony
Dr. Ice cites the following three preeminent church historians, none of whom were themselves of Premillennial persuasion and therefore none of whom wrote with prejudice, to establish the truth of the proposition we set forth here, that is, that premillennialism, far from being a recent phenomena, was actually the predominant view of the early church. Dr. Ice says, "It is generally recognized within the scholarly world of early church historians that premillennialism was the most widely held view of the earliest church tradition." I want to include quotations from three of those historians here:

> One of the leading experts on the doctrine of the early church is **J. N. D. Kelly**, who says, "millenarianism, or the theory that the returned Christ would reign on earth for a thousand years,

came to find increasing support among Christian teachers. . . . This millenarian, or 'chiliastic', doctrine was widely popular at this time." "The great theologians who followed the Apologists, Irenaeus, Tertullian and Hippolytus, were primarily concerned to defend the traditional eschatological scheme against Gnosticism," explains Kelly. "They are all exponents of millenarianism."

Philip Schaff, the dean of American church historians and himself a postmillennialist, provided the following summary of the early church's view of the millennium: "The most striking point in the eschatology of the ante-Nicene age is the prominent chiliasm, or millenarianism, that is the belief of a visible reign of Christ in glory on earth with the risen saints for a thousand years, before the general resurrection and judgment. It was indeed not the doctrine of the church embodied in any creed or form of devotion, but a widely current opinion of distinguished teachers, such as Barnabas, Papias, Justin Martyr, Irenaeus, Tertullian, Methodius, and Lactantius."

European scholar and church historian, **Adolph Harnack** tells us, "First in point of time came the faith in the nearness of Christ's second advent and the establishing of His reign of glory on the earth. Indeed it appears so early that it might be questioned whether it ought not to be regarded as an essential part of the Christian religion."

The Earliest Premillennialists

- **The Gospel writers,** especially Matthew (with his Jewish emphasis) and Luke (a companion of the Apostle Paul) had much to say about the imminent return of Christ and the Kingdom.

- **The Apostles Peter, John, James, Jude, and Paul** all wrote of Christ's coming and the things which would follow from which we derive the Premillennial understanding of eschatology.

- **Papias** (A.D. 60–130) the bishop of Hierapolis in Phrygia, Asia Minor (one of the earliest church fathers that had heard the Apostle John). Papias "related that they had heard from John how the Lord used to teach in regard to these things. Papias is recorded as saying: "there will be a millennium after the resurrection from the dead, when the personal reign of Christ will be established on this earth." Along with his witness could be cited **Polycarp** (A.D. 70–155), bishop of Smyrna and disciple of the Apostle John; **Clement of Rome,** who wrote a letter to an early church around A.D. 95; **Ignatius of Antioch,** a disciple of the Apostles John and Peter and **Theophilus of Antioch** (A.D. 115–181), who wrote one of the first accounts of primitive church history and affirmed their millennial persuasions.

- *The **Epistle of Barnabas*** (written between A.D. 120–150) presents the common belief in the second coming of Christ with the clear implication that He will set up the thousand year kingdom on earth, followed by the eight day or the eternal state.

- **Justin Martyr** (A.D. 100–165) in his *Dialogue With Trypho* (A.D. 140), a Jewish man, quoted the Apostle John as follows: "there was a certain man with us, whose name was John, one of the apostles of Christ, who prophesied, by a revelation that was made to him, that those who believed in our Christ would dwell a thousand years in Jerusalem; and that thereafter the general, and, in short, the eternal resurrection and judgment of all men would likewise take place."

- **Irenaeus** (A.D. 160–230) grew up in Asia Minor and was discipled by Polycarp, who knew the Apostle John. Irenaeus had a very extensive view of Bible prophecy.

- **Tertullian,** (contemporary of Irenaeus) makes his premillennialism clear when he says the following:

  "But we do confess that a kingdom is promised to us upon the earth, although before heaven, only in another state of existence; inasmuch as it will be after the resurrection for a thousand years in the divinely-built city of Jerusalem, "let down from heaven," which the apostle also calls "our mother from above;" and, while declaring that our citizenship is in heaven, he predicts of it that it is really a city in heaven. This both Ezekiel had knowledge of and the Apostle John beheld."

- **Lactntius** (A.D. 250–330) of North Africa. He wrote *The Divine Institutes*, which included a section on prophecy. Lactntius writes:

  "But when the thousand years shall be completed, the world shall be renewed by God, and the heavens shall be folded together, and the earth shall be changed, and God shall transform men into the similitude of angels, and they shall be white as snow; and they shall always be employed in the sight of the Almighty, and shall make offerings to their Lord, and serve Him for ever."

- Others of this period of whom we know little but who were reputed to hold to a Premillennial faith were **Tatian of Assyria,** who died in A.D. 167; **Melito, Bishop of Sardis,** who died in A.D. 170; **Clemens Alexandrinus,** who was a contemporary of Justin Martyr; **Hippolytus,** a disciple of Irenaeus, was martyred in A.D. 230 for his faith; **Victorinus, Bishop of Pettau** who died in A.D. 303; **Nepos** (an Egyptian bishop of the third century); **Cyprian, Bishop of Carthage** was martyred in A.D. 258; and **Commodians,** a Christian historian, who wrote about A.D. 250.

- **Methodius, Bishop of Tyre** died in A.D. 311 was a well know exponent of Premillennialism.

The Eclipse of Premillennialism

After this there is a gap in being able to trace expressions of the early premillennial faith. Historically this marks the institutionalization of the church under Constantine (300 AD). With the suzerainty of the bishops which developed at this time and the influences of Origen Adamantius Bishop of Alexandria (185 – 232) and St. Augustine Bishop of Hippo (354 - 430), two major changes came in the understanding of Scripture and the role of the church in history.

First, Origen developed the allegorical method by which he sought to obtain the "spiritual sense" of the text, thus allowing the words of Scripture to be at the mercy of the imagination of the interpreter. As a result the plain sense of words like *Israel, Zion, David's Throne, one thousand years*, all became subject to reinterpretation.

The second phenomena was the concept, promulgated by Augustine in his seminal work, *The City of God*, that the visible church is synonymous to the Kingdom and thus the church holds both ecclesiastical and civil authority on earth. These two erroneous ideas, created the backdrop for the dark ages, the Crusades, and all the political intrigues of the next thousand years. They are, regrettably the philosophical framework that forms the basis for the denial of premillennial truth to this day.

The Rebirth of Premillennialism

But truth is never without a witness as subsequent events testify. So we will pick up our line of Premillennialists at this point.

- **Joachim of Fiore** (1130 – 1202) In the twelfth century a new order of monks was established which spent their time in the careful pursuit of the Scriptures. The Order was founded and lead by a man we know as Joachim of Fiore and was known as the Florensian Order. Among his other convictions, Joachim wrote an entire book on the conversion of Israel. He saw history in the form of dispensations that moved on to a climax in Christ's eventual reign. Joachim wrote of the *Great Tribulation* and was the first to draw charts of dispensational periods.

- **John Olivi** (1248 – 1298) wrote ***Postilla in Apocalypsim*** a prophetic look at the future with pre-millennial perspectives.

- **Berthold of Ratisbon** (1220? – 1270?) preached the prophetic Scriptures in Germany.

- **Arnold of Villanova** (1240 – 1312) was known for his preaching of the imminent return of Christ.

- **John Wycliffe** (1324—1384) returned to a literal interpretation of all Scripture including prophecy.

- **John Huss** (1369 – 1415), priest, philosopher, reformer, and master at Charles University. Huss held a literal view of prophetic Scripture.

- **Martin Luther** (1483 - 1546) Reformer who believed the Pope was the Anti-Christ and would be destroyed at Christ's coming.

- **Andreas Karlstadt** (1480 – 1541) was an associate of Luther and ardent student who held strong views on the literal interpretation of prophecy.

- **Menno Simons** (1496 – 1561) Ana-Baptist leader who looked for Christ's imminent return and preached a pre-millennial faith.

- **Philipp Jakob Spener** (1635 – 1705) The University of Halle was founded under his influence in 1694 and later became the greatest missionary force of its day. The only two points on which he departed from the orthodox Lutheran faith were the requirement of regeneration as the *sine qua non* of the true theologian, and the expectation of the conversion of the Jews and the fall of Papacy as the prelude of the triumph of the church. Spener was one of the godfathers of Count von Zinzendorf, the leader of the Moravian Brethren's Community at Herrnhut in Saxony.

- **Thomas Draxe** (died 1618) was an Anglican divine and an authoritative theological and classical author. He wrote a commentary on Romans 11 that argued for Israel's restoration based upon his Covenant Theology.

- **Thomas Brightman** (1552-1607) was an English clergyman and Puritan Bible commentator. His work *Shall They Return to Jerusalem Again?* advocated for the return of the Jews to the Holy Land.

- **Joseph Mede** (1586-1638) was a Puritan, biblical scholar, Egyptologist, Hebraist, and the father of English pre-millennialism. His writings advocated strongly for a restoration of the Jewish people to their homeland.

- **Henry Finch** (1558-1625) was a Member of the British Parliament, Puritan, jurist and legal scholar. His seminal work, *The World's Great Restoration*, published in 1621, is considered to be the first clearly articulated plan for restoration of the Jewish nation. Finch taught that the biblical passages that describe a return of the Jews to their own land should be taken literally, not as allegorical references to the Church.

- **Isaac de La Peyrere** (1594-1676) was a Huguenot, the French Ambassador to Denmark, and the leader of a large Christian group in France. La Peyrere wrote a book entitled, *Rappel des Juifs*, which called for the "Restoration of Israel as the Jewish nation in the Holy Land." He sent this treatise to the French government.

- **Oliver Cromwell** (1599-1658) led the English Revolution, and ruled the Commonwealth of Britain as Lord Protector. He said, "And it may be, as some think, God will bring the Jews home to their station, 'from all the isles of the sea,' and answer their expectations 'as from the depths of the sea.'"

- **Anders Pederson Kempe** (1622-1689) was a German theologian. In his book, *Israel's Good News,* he wrote, "You Christians, you let yourselves be persuaded by false teachers, ... to believe that the Jews were forever disinherited and rejected by God and that you were now the rightful Christian Israel, to possess the Land of Canaan forever."

- **Increase Mather** (1639-1723) was a Puritan leader and a major figure in the founding of the Massachusetts Bay Colony who wrote more than 100 books over the course of his lifetime, the first of which was, *The Mystery of Israel's Salvation.* Like many of America's earliest founders, Mather carried a strong belief in Israel's restoration - a feeling that has remained deeply embedded in the Nation's culture ever since.

- **John Milton** (1608-1674) was an English poet and scholar, who wrote of Israel's restitution in his celebrated *Paradise Regained.* He wrote, "Yet He at length, time to himself best know remembering Abraham, by some wondrous call may bring them back." *De Doctrina Christiana* - which was not published until nearly 150 years after Milton's death - provides further evidence of the author's millenarian convictions and belief in Israel's revival.

- **John Tolland** (1670-1722) was an Irish participant in England's theological and political debates. In 1714, he published *Reasons for Naturalizing the Jews in Great Britain and Ireland on the Same Footing with all Other Nations*. This work paved the way for Jews to enter Parliament.

- **Isaac Newton** (1642-1727) was a world-famous 17th century scientist, who first defined gravity and revolutionized mankind's understanding of physics. Newton studied Hebrew and believed the prophecies in the Old Testament about the Jews' return to Israel. He thought that the rebuilding of Jerusalem would take place in the late 19th century, and that the Temple would be rebuilt in the 20th or 21st century.

- **Nikolaus Zinzendorf** (1700-1760) was a German pietist and the Bishop of the Moravian Church. He oversaw the Moravian Church's revival, making it the first church to send out missionaries around the world. Although he emphasized missions and evangelism, Zinzendorf exhibited great respect for the Jewish people and sought to prepare the Moravian church for an imminent mass conversion of Jews.

- **Joseph Priestley** (1733-1804) was a famous chemist who discovered oxygen. An ardent Zionist, he was quoted as saying, "the God of Heaven, the God of Abraham, Isaac and Jacob whom we Christians as well as you worship, may be graciously pleased to put an end to your suffering, gathering you from all nations, resettle you in your own country, the land of Canaan and make you the most illustrious...of all nations on the earth."

- **Johann Heinrich Jung-Stilling** (1740-1817) was a famous eye specialist and pietist. In his influential book, *Das Heimweh von Heinrich Stilling*, Jung-Stilling wrote, "God has proclaimed through the prophets of old that the people of Israel would be scattered throughout the world. Who can deny that this has taken place? Yet the same prophets have prophesied that in the latter days God would gather his people again from the four corners of the earth, and bring them back to the land which he promised to their fathers long ago to be an everlasting possession....The land of Palestine will again become the possession of the Jewish people."

- **Joseph Eyre** (1754-1803) was an English Evangelical leader and clergyman who founded a number of Evangelical institutions, such as The Evangelical Magazine and the London Missionary Society. He drew public attention to the ancient biblical promises that God made to Abraham, publishing *Observations upon Prophecies Relating to the Restoration of the Jews*.

- **John Wesley** (1703-1791) was an Anglican cleric credited with founding the Methodist denomination. His preaching notes on Romans 11:12 say "So many prophecies refer to this grand event, that it is surprising any Christian can doubt it. And these are greatly confirmed by the wonderful preservation of the Jews as a distinct people to this day. When it is accomplished, it will be a strong a demonstration, both of the Old and New Testament revelation...."

- **Charles Wesley** (1707-1788) the brother of John Wesley, was the leader of the Methodist movement, and the author of more than 6,000 hymns. He wrote about the restoration of Israel in the hymn *Almighty God of Love* based on Isaiah 66:19-20 and Romans 11:26: "We know it must be done, For God hath spoke the word...rebuilt by His command Jerusalem shall rise...send then thy servants forth to call the Hebrews home, From west and east, and south, and north, let all the wanderers come." It is many of Wesley's hymns that Sabeel now seeks to strike from the hymnbook (see Foreword).

- **Charles Jerram** (1770-1853) was an English Evangelical clergyman who wrote a prominent essay on the scriptural grounds for expecting the future restoration of the Jewish people to their land.

- **Thomas Newton** (1704-1782) was an English cleric, biblical scholar, and author, who served as the Bishop of Bristol. He believed that the Jews would be restored to their native land. In *Dissertations On The Prophecies,* (1754), he wrote "The Jews are by a constant miracle preserved a distinct people for the completion of the other prophecies relating to them."

Premillennialism in the 1800s

- **Lord Shaftesbury (Anthony Ashley Cooper)** (1801-1885) was an influential English politician, philanthropist, and one of the main proponents of Christian Zionism during the Victorian Era. In 1839 Shaftesbury published, *The State and the rebirth of the Jews* - an article that urged the Jews to return to Palestine and occupy the lands of Galilee and Judea. His efforts helped to convince Lord Palmerston - the British Foreign Secretary at the time - to try and persuade the Turkish Sultan to allow significant Jewish immigration to Palestine.

- **Robert Browning** (1812-1889) was a well-known English poet - and an expert in Jewish literature, who often read the Old Testament in the original Hebrew. He wrote in 1855, in *The Holy Cross Day*, "The Lord will have mercy on Jacob yet, And again in his border see Israel yet, When Judah beholds Jerusalem, The strangers shall be joined to them; To Jacob's House shall the Gentiles cleave, So the Prophet sayeth and the sons believe."

- **George Eliot** (1819-1880) was the pen name of author Mary Anne Evans - a famous English novelist and Evangelical Christian - who loved, supported, and encouraged Jews to reestablish the State of Israel, in particular through her novel, *Daniel Deronda*. First published in 1876, this work created an iconic Zionist hero. It was the most significant literary work of Zionism written by a non-Jew, the culmination of a long tradition that dated back to the Protestant idea of Restoration.

- **Robert Murray M' Cheyne** (1813-1843) was a Presbyterian minister in the Church of Scotland, who authored a Church report along with **Andrew Bonar** on *The Condition of the Jews in their Land*. Their report was widely publicized in Great Britain. It was followed by a *Memorandum to Protestant Monarchs of Europe for the restoration of the Jews to Palestine*, which was printed verbatim in the **London Times**, igniting an enthusiastic campaign in Britain for the restoration of the Jews to their land.

- **John Nelson Darby** (1800-1882) was an Anglican clergyman who became the founder of the Plymouth Brethren - an Evangelical Christian movement that defined the doctrine of dispensational pre-millennialism. He taught that the Jews would return to their land before the second advent of Christ. While Darby did not originate the pre-millennial position, he did define it and gave it structure.

- **J.C. Ryle** (1816-1900) was the Bishop of Liverpool and one of the most authoritative Anglican leaders of the nineteenth century. In his sermon, *Scattered Israel to be Gathered,* he argued that the national restoration of Israel was so clear in scripture that denying it would be as incomprehensible as denying the divinity of Christ.

- **Charles Haddon Spurgeon** (1834 - 1892) was England's most influential preacher and one of the most widely read men of his era. In a famous sermon in 1864 on Ezekiel 37, he said, "If there is anything clear and plain, the literal sense and meaning of this passage - a meaning not to be spirited or spiritualized away - it must be evident that both the two and the ten tribes of Israel are to be restored to their own land and that a king is to rule over them."

Premillennialism in the Twentieth Century

- **John Stoddard** (1850-1931) was a famous American hymn writer who wrote in 1897: "You are a people without a country; there is a country without a people. Be united. Fulfill the dreams of your old poets and patriarchs. Go back - go back to the land of Abraham.'"

- **William H. Hechler** (1845-1931) was a British clergyman, who became a devoted friend of Theodor Herzl and a critical supporter of the early Zionists. Hechler tutored the son of the Grand Duke of Baden - the future German Emperor. He was a strong believer in biblical prophecies of the Jewish return to Israel and worked with British Christians to aid Jewish refugees from Russian pogroms.

- **Lord Arthur James Balfour** (1848-1930) was a British Prime Minister, statesman, and the author of the seminal Balfour Declaration, which was credited as the legal foundation for the creation of the State of Israel in 1948. A deeply religious man steeped in the Bible, Balfour convinced the British War Cabinet to issue the Balfour Declaration in 1917, which called for "the establishment in Palestine of a national home for the Jewish people."

- **William E. Blackstone** (1860-1929) was a Chicago businessman and Evangelical Christian, who wrote several booklets predicting the Jewish return to their land including his famous *Jesus Is Coming*. His ardent support for Zionism arose from an unwavering belief in the prophetic scriptures and a desire to see an end to Jewish persecution in Europe. In

1891, he presented President Benjamin Harrison with a petition with over 400 prominent Christian signatures calling for American support for the Jewish return. He later influenced President Woodrow Wilson to accept the Balfour Declaration.

- **President Woodrow Wilson** (1854-1924) was the U.S. President who guided American policy through World War I - and was the son, and grandson, of Presbyterian ministers. The British government refused to issue the Balfour Declaration without his support. He gave his support with reservations, concerned that there could be serious political consequences for such a declaration. Yet, he believed that returning Palestine to the Jews had divine ramifications.

- **Prime Minister Lloyd George** (1863-1945) was a British Prime Minister and statesman. Driven by sympathy and admiration of the Jews - and his life-long study of the Bible - George conducted a large-scale offensive to gain control of Palestine, in the hope that a British Mandate in Palestine could restore it to the Jews. He regarded this as God's work.

- **Lt. Col. John Henry Patterson** (1867-1947) was an Irish Protestant and Bible student who led the Zion Mule Corps - a group of Jewish volunteers who fought for Britain during WWI. He rejoiced at the Balfour Declaration and wrote: "Christians, too, have always believed in the fulfillment of prophecy and the restoration of the Jewish people...Nothing like this has been known since the days of King Cyrus."

- **Charles Orde Wingate** (1903-1944) was a British officer and devout Bible believer. In 1936, he began training the Haganah - the main military force of the Jewish community in British Palestine. He used the Hebrew scriptures as a training manual and created the night squads, which included future Israeli commanders Yigal Allon and Moshe Dayan.

- **John Grauel** (1917-1986) was a Methodist minister, who volunteered on the Exodus-1947 - a ship packed with 4,500 Holocaust survivors that was assaulted by the British en-route to Palestine. Grauel was the ship's only non-Jewish crew member.

- **William Hull** (1897-1992) was a Canadian clergyman living in Jerusalem, who helped to convince the United Nations Special Committee on Palestine (UNSCOP) to recommend the creation of a Jewish state. Reverend Hull spoke to Justice Rand about the injustices visited upon the Jewish community by both the British and the Arabs. Reverend Hull also submitted a letter to the full committee, which made the case for Biblical Zionism. UNSCOP followed the lead of Justice Rand, recommending the partition of the land into separate Jewish and Arab States. This set the stage for the creation of the State of Israel on May 14, 1948.

- **Pres. Harry S. Truman** (1884-1972) was the U.S. President whose Southern Baptist Biblical background influenced his decision to make America the first state to recognize Israel in 1948, against the advice of the State Department. When confronted with the possible retaliation of oil-rich Arab countries, he said that he would: "handle the situation in light of justice, not oil." Truman compared his role in the founding of the State to that of Cyrus, King of Persia, who enabled the Jews to return to their homeland in the sixth century BC.

As mentioned in the Foreword, this list is certainly not exhaustive and it particularly omits the names of men in this generation who have refined and defined the premillennial position to a remarkable degree.

Men like **C. I. Scofield** helped to define and popularize millennialism and Israel's future. Theologians like **Lewis Sperry Chafer, John F. Walvoord, J. Dwight Pentecost, Alva J. McClain, James M. Gray, Arthur T. Pierson, W. G. Moorehead, Arno C. Gaebelein, William L. Pettingill, H. A.**

Ironside and **Dr. Donald Grey Barnhouse** contributed much to our understanding of the Scriptural doctrine of the future.

American Theologians were not alone in their understanding of Premillennial truth. In Europe there were men like **F. B. Myer, W. Graham Scroggie,** and **Canon Harry Sutton** who wrote and preached prophetic Scriptures including the restoration and conversion of the nation of Israel. Men like **Erich Sauer** defied the Hitler regime to proclaim the truth concerning Israel's place in God's program and **Rene Pache** in Switzerland strongly supported the Premillennial position. He was also one of the founders of Intervarsity, an organization that has, alas, left the prophetic heritage he invested it with.

Today the work of men like **Dr. Charles C. Ryrie, Dr. Renald Showers, Dr. Thomas Ice, Dr. David Larsen** and **Robert Lightner** continue to wrestle with the text to give us a reasoned logical presentation of our Premillennial view, and help to present a logical defense for that position.

Finally, there are the evangelists. **Dwight L. Moody** was an ardent Premillennialist and Dispensationalist. **Charles E. Fuller** won more people to Christ through his messages on the Rapture than any other subject, and evangelist **Billy Graham** has steadfastly maintained his belief in Christ's imminent coming throughout his ministry.

The value of the forgoing list lies in two things: First, it should be noted that each of those whose names appear held the convictions they did because of a reverence and respect for the inspired words of Scripture. They interpreted Scripture in its literal grammatical and historical sense and formed their opinions and actions based upon it.

The second value it has is that it should inform our understanding sufficiently that we will not be deceived by the myth that "the teaching of an imminent return of Jesus Christ for the Church, the restoration and conversion of the nation Israel, and the earthly, glorious reign of Jesus Christ over this earth for a thousand years is the late concoction of J.N. Darby (1800 – 1882), and a few of his followers in the nineteenth century."

That fable should be forever put to rest by the abundance of the evidence. These truths have been held by sound biblical scholars through the ages, and they have their basis in the writings of the Apostles themselves. Those of us who ascribe to them not only have Scripture on our side, but a veritable and venerable cloud of witnesses.

Bibliography

SECTION ONE: THE CERTAINTY OF ISRAEL'S CONVERSION

1. Susan Michael; (Article); Jerusalem Connection Feb. 19, 2014, critique of *Zionism Unsettled.*

2. *Christian Zionism, Road-map to Armageddon?* Inter Varsity Press. 2004

3. Charles (Chuck) Carlson http://charlesecarlson.com/

4. Dr. John Hagee; *In Defense of Israel*; U-Tube

5. Jonathan Burnis; *The Dangers of Dual Covenant Theology*; Charisma Magazine 8/7/2009

6. C. H. Spurgeon; *The Spurgeon Collection, Metropolitan Pulpit*, X, 1864 no. 582: 533, 536-37

7. Dwight Pentecost; *Things to Come*; Dunham Publishing Co. 1958, pp72

8. Ibid. pp. 97

9. John F. Walvoord, Roy B. Zuck, Bible Knowledge Commentary; Cook 2004 E-Sword

10. J. C. Ryle, *Are You Ready for the End of Time?* (Fearn Scotland: Christian Focus, 2001) pp 183; (reprint of *Coming Events and Present Duties*)

11. Barry Horner; *Future Israel*; B&H Academic, Nashville, Tenn. pp.255

12.   Scofield Reference Bible; Oxford University Press 1917; footnote, pp. 1202

13.   Ibid. pp. 75

14.   Albert Barnes; *Notes on the Bible*; E-Sword

15.   Dr. Thomson; *Land and the Book, Lebanon, Damascus and Beyond Jordon;* pp 35 (cited by Vincent)

16.   R.E. Diprose; *Israel and the Church*; Authentic Media; Waynesboro, GA 2000; pp 20 – 21.

17.   Jonathan Edwards; *A History of the Work of Redemption*, vol. 9 ed. John F. Wilson (New Haven: Yale University Press, 1989; pp 469.

SECTION TWO: THE CIRCUMSTANCES OF ISRAEL'S CONVERSION

18.   Scofield Reference Bible; Oxford University Press 1917; footnote pp 53

19.   Ibid. footnote pp. 43

20.   V. Raymond Edman; *The Disciplines of Life*; Kregel; poem, *When God Makes a Man* pp. 54

21.   Stanley Ellison *Who Owns the Land?* Portland: Multnomah 1991 pp 186; (cited by Barry Horner; *Future Israel*; B&H Academic, Nashville, Tenn. pp. 365

22.   Dwight Pentecost; *Things to Come;* Dunham Publishing Co. 1958, pp 344 – 350

23.   Ibid. pp. 327

24.   Josephus; *Antiquities of the Jews Book I Chapter 6*

25. Ibid. pp.328 sites William Kelly, *Notes on Ezekiel*, London: G. Morrish pp. 192, 193

26. Sale Harrison; *The Coming Great Northern Confederacy*, Hephzibah House pp. 16-17.

27. Ibid. 328

28. Compton's Encyclopedia, Volume 8, pp. 248

29. Edward Gibbon; *Decline and Fall of the Roman Empire*; volume 1, pp 204

30. Dwight Pentecost; *Things to Come;* Dunham Publishing Co. 1958, op. cit., pp. 33.

31. Israel's Wealth; Wikipedia Foundation; www.en.wikipedia.org

32. Commentary on the Old Testament; Keil & Delitzsch; E-Sword.

33. Earthquake/tsunami from UNESCO (trace) USGS; Wikipedia Foundation; www.en.wikipedia.org

34. John F. Walvoord, Roy B. Zuck, Bible Knowledge Commentary; *Ezekiel,* Cook 2004 E-Sword

35. Ibid.

36. John F. Walvoord, Roy B. Zuck, Bible Knowledge Commentary; *Joel,* Cook 2004 E-Sword

37. John F. Walvoord, Roy B. Zuck, Bible Knowledge Commentary; *Joel,* Cook 2004 E-Sword

38. Earthquakes; This report has been based on data available from USGS (NEIC) and other online sources, such as Wikipedia, in an attempt to cover as much of the available data as possible.

SECTION THREE: THE CONSQUENCES & CHALLENGES OF ISRAEL'S CONVERSION

39. Lehman Strauss; *The Book of Revelation*; Loizeaux Brothers, pp. 175

40. Author: Malthie D. Babcock/composer: Franklin L. Sheppard; *This Is My Father's World*; (Public Domain)

41. Dwight Pentecost; *Things to Come;* Dunham Publishing Co. 1958, pp

42. Scofield Reference Bible; Oxford University Press 1917; footnote pp 920

43. Appendix I Abba Eban; Interview 1958

44. Appendix II Sources:
    - David Larsen; *Company of Hope;* (DLL Pub.);
    - Thomas Ice: *A Brief History Of Early Premillennialism;* http://www.pre-trib.org/data/pdf/Ice-ABriefHistoryofEarly.pdf;
    - *Israel Answers*; http://www.israelanswers.com/christian_zionism/a_history_of_christian_zionism

About the Author:

Born in Altoona, Pennsylvania, Dr. Shade completed studies at Philadelphia Bible Institute and Wheaton College. He began serving in faith missionary work in 1956 with *Scripture Memory Mountain Mission* in Southeastern Kentucky, where he regularly ministered to 10,000 teenagers in seven counties through the high school ministry. During the same time, he became pastor of McRoberts Missionary Baptist Church where he served for eight years.

In 1964, Dr. Shade moved to York, Pennsylvania, where he founded and directed the *Grace and Truth Evangelistic Association* which was active in radio and television ministry, evangelistic campaigns, and conference / camp ministries. He was the founder and director of *Teen Encounter*, *Camp of the Nations* and *Wayside Maternity Home* for unwed mothers. He also directed the project of preparing curriculum for *World-Wide Bible Institutes*, which organizes Bible institutes in local churches and mission stations around the world. During this time he received his Doctorate (DD), from Toledo Bible College & Seminary.

Dr Shade has served for eighteen years with *Source of Light Ministries International*, eight years as General Director. He now serves as Director of Advanced Studies Department which administers both the *WWBI* program and *Ezra Institute.* Ruby has served along with her husband in every place and project. The Shades continue actively serving with SLM in Bible teaching, evangelism and conference ministry both in this country and abroad.

BY THE SAME AUTHOR:

Amazed by Grace, the book that tells of God's marvelous faithfulness and miraculous acts in the life and ministry of Dr. Bill & Ruby Shade, is available in bookstores and on Amazon now.

You can order a copy at a considerable saving now and receive, in addition a CD copy of the Unshackled dramatization of the Shade's ministry with your copy of the book.

To order your copy through Pay-Pal go to:

http://www.amazedbygracebook.com

Made in the USA
Charleston, SC
17 June 2014